Gabe Segoine's *Surfing North Korea* is a colorful, personal memoir of faith-based humanitarian, developmental, and tourism work in North Korea, among the first of its kind. From drilling wells to surfing waves, Segoine offers a wealth of details about life, society, and government in the oft-described *hermit kingdom*. He is truly a peacemaker in every sense of the word. Highly readable and recommended for students and scholars interested in North Korea and humanitarian organizations.

JOSEPH YI

ASSOCIATE PROFESSOR OF POLITICAL SCIENCE
HANYANG UNIVERSITY, SEOUL, SOUTH KOREA

Surfing North Korea is a MUST read for anyone wanting to visit or to engage with North Korea. From his wealth of experience through tourism and humanitarian work, Gabe Segoine outlines the dos and don'ts when visiting the country, but more importantly he advocates for positive and relational engagement with the local people. Having lived and worked in North Korea for 11 years ourselves, Gabe is one of only a few people we would trust to write a book like this. He accurately describes the real-world situation on the ground. Stereotypes and misconceptions about North Korea are shattered, as Gabe shares from personal, firsthand experience. Using his innovative approach of surfing to engage with the people, his life experience opens up the minds of readers in how to engage with North Koreans.

STEPHEN AND JOY Y~~~~

FIELD DIF

D1310435

Surfing in North Korea? Going to North Korea through its front gates? Doing business in North Korea? Such concepts would never have crossed my mind before I met Gabe Segoine and heard his story of engagement in this secretive nation. Like many people, my thoughts of North Korea were of doom and gloom and a country where engagement was impossible. By no means does Gabe's journey minimize the challenges faced there, but you can't help opening up your mind to the possibility of hope, peace and even unification on the Korean Peninsula if more people like him had the courage, curiosity, fortitude, creativity, heart and faith to treat the other not as an enemy but as chingu or friend.

HYEPIN IM
PRESIDENT/CEO
FAITH & COMMUNITY EMPOWERMENT (FACE)
LOS ANGELES, CALIFORNIA, USA

Surfing North Korea And Other Stories from Inside comes at a perfect time when North Korea desires to normalize its relationship with the rest of the world. Be ready to be blown out of your mind as Gabe Segoine details some of his own and others' experiences inside the country. It's a no nonsense type of book from someone who has spent extensive time inside the country as an American. He gives a brutally straight-talk that everyone, especially American and South Koreans, ought to read if they want to understand North Korea and want to engage its people. Since his engagement with North Korea is so extensive and invested, Segoine gives a fresh inside-outside perspective that you would not get anywhere else. This is a must-read if you are thinking of ever visiting North Korea.

JAMIE KIM
FOUNDER/DIRECTOR OF REAH INTERNATIONAL

I tell people we are going surfing in North Korea and the response is always "You mean South Korea." No, North Korea! You ask how is this possible? It's because of one man's faith, vision and passion, Gabe Segoine. Gabe's book *Surfing North Korea* is a documentary of just how powerful the sport of surfing is in influencing the people and future culture of North Korea. The decision to GO is all it takes. To personally witness this for four years with Gabe and see the "stoke" on the faces of new North Korean surfers makes you want to return and believe that nothing is impossible. Thank you Gabe for encouraging us to invest and plant seeds of greatness, you have made surfing history.

TOM BAUER

CO-FOUNDER

SURFING THE NATIONS

Surfing North Korea

And Other Stories from Inside

Gabe Segoine

Surfing North Korea And Other Stories from Inside

Published by the Klug Publishing Group, LLC
Copyright © 2018 by Gabe Segoine.

Printed in the United States of America.

Some names and identifying details have been changed
to protect the privacy of individuals.

First Edition

ISBN 978-0-9995870-2-7

Surfing North Korea And Other Stories from Inside is a publication of the:

Klug Publishing Group, LLC
1136 Union Mall Ste 301
Honolulu, HI 96813-2711

Cover design by HACKnTOG LLC.

Cover photo by Bridget Butler.

Photos contributed by:
Bridget Butler
Gabe Segoine
Keith Bitting
Dee Jess
Graham Williams
Tom Bauer
Karlan Kim
Paul Kim
Iris Kim

www.surfingnorthkorea.com

For Keith Michael Bitting
who fought the good fight and never lost hope
for a peaceful and unified Korea.

"If we can introduce surfing to North Korea,
then anything is possible."

Contents

Foreword. 13

Preface 17

Introduction. 21

Why Engagement Matters. 27

Traveling to North Korea 41

Humanitarian Work 61

Well Drilling. 85

Engagement Through Tourism 111

Breaking Down Walls 137

Surfing Diplomacy 159

Sharing Our Culture 185

Lasting Impact 209

Endnotes. .233

Foreword

On April 27, 2018, the world witnessed a historic moment when the two Korean leaders met face-to-face for the first time in decades. South Korean President Moon Jae In and North Korean leader Kim Jong Un held hands as they crossed over into each other's countries by walking over the DMZ line — the line that has symbolized the separation of a nation that has been at war for the past 65 years. I was in tears as I watched the video over and over again in disbelief that this was really happening, as I have had the privilege of standing on both sides of the DMZ.

For those of us who have been studying the delicate situation for the past several decades, we understand that there are significant gaps to close in terms of perception and understanding both within the two Koreas and with the broader international community. Within the two Koreas, significant education and awareness building will be critical to ensure a smooth transition into a truly unified "One Korea." Each side has been told very different stories of what is happening on the other side. Each side has different points of view on the idea of reunification. Each side has been victim somewhat to the political rhetoric they have been exposed to. Despite all the orotundity and "brainwashing," I believe the sentiment shared with me by a North Korean guard summarizes the deeper emotional desires of many as he held my hand, looked at me (a Korean-American) and said, "We are the same people."

On the international front, the knowledge and perception gaps are even wider, as the majority of news we have received about the North has centered around nuclear proliferation, trade sanctions, and "power grabbing." This is due in large part because the "hermit kingdom" has been effective at limiting what gets in and out of their country. Very few outsiders have even had the opportunity to learn what it's like to live inside the country, how it actually works, who the people are, what motivates them and what the developments have been. Gabe is one of those few.

All that is about to change. The future has never been more exciting for the idea of a "One Korea." We will need to develop clear transformation roadmaps with key stakeholders including policy makers, humanitarian workers, cultural experts, business, educators and civil society (and maybe a few surfers). It will require us to start with understanding, empathy and having an open mind towards the people and country of North Korea.

There is no one I know that is more qualified to help close some of these perception gaps. Through over a decade of serving the people in North Korea over 19 trips, Gabe is one of the few foreigners who has been able to earn the trust of local leaders and execute successful engagement strategies across business, humanitarian work, and cultural exchange. Through each story, prepare to be challenged and inspired by what's possible. Who knew that one day, we would be surfing in the most closed country in the world? But it happened in 2014. Gabe inspires us with what's possible when people engage in very human ways.

Given the road ahead, there could not have been a better time for this book than now. As Gabe takes you on a journey of truly remarkable things that have been happening through effective engagement strategies, I challenge you to keep an open mind and heart towards the people of North Korea who are just as human as you and I. It's time for a new narrative.

So Young Kang
Founder & CEO, Gnowbe
Founding Partner, Awaken Group
LNKM Board Member
May 1, 2018

Preface

My first visit to North Korea[1] was in 2007. I've since made 19 trips in various capacities, from (Non-Governmental Organization) NGO humanitarian relief work, to helping set up a for-profit well drilling business, as well as leading sports and cultural exchange tours, which are a main topic of this book.

My studies on North Korea began in 1999, and since then, I've read many books on the subject, as well as watched many videos and documentaries. North Korean news feeds fill my inbox daily. My South Korean-born wife has also helped immensely expand my understanding and knowledge of Korean culture.

I've traveled throughout a large portion of North Korea and visited areas from the capital Pyongyang, to other provincial cities, to small rural villages where I've been involved with clean water projects. I personally know people from many levels of society, from government officials to local water well-drilling workers, to many other local people with whom I've come to know along my travels, and some I even count as friends.

By no means do I consider myself an expert on Korea as I don't profess to grasp all there is to know about the country. In fact, there is much we, on the outside, still do not know about North Korea. Of course, there are people who know a lot about the country, either from study or experience on the ground or both. These might be considered "experts" to some extent. I believe that only North Koreans are the real experts on their country.

There's enough blame to go around regarding the ongoing strife in Korea, and so I've done my best to keep blame to a minimum, and instead focused on my philosophy for engaging North Korea. This philosophy may be considered radical by some or even useless by others, but trying to satisfy everyone is an unattainable goal. The inter-Korean situation is incredibly complex, and people hold many differing positions. I don't pretend to have all the answers to a problem of such great complexity. My hope, is that by writing down my engagement philosophy, and my experiences, this book might offer, even in some small way, a positive contribution towards the narrative surrounding North Korea and inter-korean relations.

My Christian faith holds a major part of my life, and is not something I can completely separate from my experiences in the Democratic People's Republic of Korea or DPRK as it is formally known. My personal faith and religious beliefs are not the focus of this book but are definitely an underlying factor. However, in order to reach the broadest audience possible, this book instead focuses on my philosophy and experiences of engaging the people of North Korea.

To be clear, my position is not "pro North Korea" nor is it "pro American" or even "pro South Korea." It is pro "One Korea" or as my friend and co-worker Peter calls it, "New Korea," which is a Korean peninsula living in long-term peace and prosperity.

This book represents my views based on my personal experiences as well as those of people close to me. This book cannot deal with all sides of the story, nor is it intended to. Since there is so much more to the picture than I can cover in the following pages, my assumption is that if the reader finds the subject of North Korea of interest, they will do their own research into other aspects of the country.

For the purpose of security, I have selectively changed the names of both foreign field workers working inside North Korea, as well as those of North Korean workers with whom I've had working relationships.

Introduction

My sisters and I grew up riding in the back of a 1966 Volkswagen van. You see, our parents were hippies, not the smelly, cover up your stench with patchouli oil kind, but the clean living, health oriented make the world a better place kind. To them, the only "race" on earth is the "human race," which instilled in my sisters and me the idea that people are all equal no matter their color, social status or age.

We lived in a small mountain town in Southern California. I remember one night when I was 11 or 12 watching my dad play in the local basketball league. A fight broke out and my dad stepped in between two players who were pretty close to throwing punches. He said, "Come on now brothers, there's no need to fight, it's only a game," and he was able to appease the situation. Of course, those two guys weren't really his "brothers," that's just how my dad referred to them because to him we are all "brothers and sisters," part of the "brotherhood of man." My dad always seemed to be the guy who would step into the middle of a fight in order to bring peace. I guess this is partially from where my heart for being a peacemaker came.

My interest in Korea really started with the popular American television show M.A.S.H. As a child, I had no real understanding about the actual situation on the Korean Peninsula or the Korean War, but it was fascinating to watch how these doctors on the show were in Korea to help save lives. This very subtle interest in Korea carried on into my adulthood.

My first trip to South Korea was in 1997, as part of a church group. When we first boarded Korean Airlines, all the young men in my group were struck by the beauty of the flight attendants. I was single at the time and agreed they were some of the most beautiful women I'd ever seen, which might help to explain why I eventually married a Korean woman.

We served at a local Korean church in the port city of Busan. One thing I observed about Korean people is how amazingly hospitable they are. The people and culture were really interesting. The Korean locals who hosted my group did an incredible job treating us to amazing local foods and showing us around the city. More importantly though, one of our Korean hosts told me all there was to know about the North Korean famine, which at the time was really severe. From the media coverage, we knew there was a famine occurring but we didn't have any real details. He also told me about the national division of Korea, as well as his desire to one day see the two united into one new Korea. This was an important point in my understanding of how Korea became divided, and the beginning of a hope that one day there might come a time of healing.

After my trip, I returned to Hawaii where I was living at that time, and began to study more about North Korea, Korean history, the Korean War and the issues surrounding national division. All of these things taken together gave me a desire to somehow become part, even if only in some small way, of the solution and healing of a divided Korea.

My wife, Joy, is from South Korea and came to Hawaii for English studies in 1999. After finding out she also had an interest in North Korea, as well as a passion for reunification, I began to pursue a relationship. We married in 2000 and began planning to move to Korea, to begin working towards national unification. After having three beautiful daughters, we moved to Korea in 2006, where my work inside North Korea began.

To be honest, writing a book about my experiences in North Korea was not high on my to-do list. My lovely wife has been urging me for years, "You gotta write a book, you gotta do it soon!" To which I'd reply, "Yeah, yeah, I'm writing it in my head. I'll get to it someday!"

I recently felt compelled to write it all down. Maybe it was simply just the right time, as the Korean

Peninsula has recently experienced quite possibly the highest tensions since the Korean War. It might be the opportune time for new ideas and strategies for bringing about peace to be disseminated.

Why Engagement Matters

Historical Context

Korea is a country with a long and fascinating, yet often sad history. The current status on the Korean Peninsula is one of division. Prior to the modern era, Korea was united under the Chosun Dynasty. The dynasty came to an official end in the early part of the twentieth century, as the Japanese began to exert influence on the Korean peninsula. In 1907, Japan began to take control of Korean internal policy, and by 1910, they annexed Korea as a colony. It was in this context of Japanese occupation of the Korean peninsula where Kim Il Sung began his rise in the ranks as a "freedom fighter" against the occupation.

When we think about North Korea today, it's important that we understand that they'll never agree to the concept of occupation. They see the U.S. and U.N. forces in South Korea as occupiers, an idea which goes back to the era of Japanese occupation. Another consideration is that initially, national division was not something the Korean people chose for themselves. With the end of World War II and the removal of Japanese control, Russia wanted to exercise its influence over the Korean Peninsula. Of course, the United States wanted to counter this, and it was these two superpowers who bisected the Korean Peninsula along the 38th parallel.

By the end of the war Kim Il Sung had risen in the ranks and under Russian influence became the leader of the North. With the North under Communist Russian influence and the South under the influence of the United States, the Korean Peninsula became officially divided in 1948. The Korean War then began in 1950, lasting until 1953. With the cessation of war, major fighting ended at the 38th parallel.

Although Russia and the U.S. unofficially divided the Peninsula, it is important to remember that after World War II ended, the Korean people did not chose to be divided; instead it was thrust upon them. Unfortunately, this division has lasted until today, with a cease-fire in place between the North and South and an armistice between North Korea and the U.S. and U.N. forces stationed on the Peninsula. For more than 60 years North Korea and South Korea have been officially at war, with Korean brothers continually and ceaselessly pointing guns at each other across the

Demilitarized Zone or DMZ, 365 days a year, year after year after year.

Kim Jong Un Is Their Leader

Because of his reputation, people often ask me if the current leader of North Korea is "crazy." Since I've traveled there quite a few times, it seems people think I somehow know him personally. So let me clear that up by stating I've never met Kim Jong Un or even seen him in person. That's not to say if I had the opportunity to meet him, I wouldn't take it.

What I know about Kim Jong Un is what everybody else knows about him from the media. The only thing I'd add are the things I've heard about him from local people on the ground in North Korea. From my observations, the man and his government are very much in control. Their decisions, whether we agree with them or not, are made for specific, rational (in their view), calculated purposes with specific long-term goals in mind. Understanding this fact would greatly help in our overall understanding of why the leadership of North Korea does what it does.

But many will ask if they're trying to start a war. The short answer is: no I don't believe they want war. The North Korean leadership understands very well that war is the worst possible scenario for all parties. They put a lot of importance in their nuclear program using the same rationale other governments might use, but I don't believe that their intent is ever to use it for a preemptive nuclear strike. Kim Jong Un and those around him understand that a nuclear war doesn't end well for anyone.

President Donald Trump was noted to have called Kim Jong Un "a pretty smart cookie."[2] When Kim Jong Un first took over the position of leadership, many people thought that he would not last long. Every year, I'd hear supposed experts saying that he wouldn't last; yet here he is, still in power. The fact is, he's been able to survive as their leader in spite of his young age and in spite of sanctions and isolation. He even outlasted the former South Korean President Park Geun Hye, who was impeached before her five-year term was up. There really isn't any reason why he wouldn't continue in power if he stays in good health. This is not in any way a defense or endorsement of his leadership and decisions.

There may be people who won't like these observations, but we have to come to grips with reality. If we are ever going to see long-term solutions, we need to engage North Korea where they are, which is with Kim Jong Un as their leader. Policies based on where they were 10 years ago, or based on where we wish they would be are doomed to failure. When we talk about a path forward, at least for the foreseeable future, we should assume that path will go through the Kim Jong Un government.

The Value of Engagement Through Tourism

There is a prevailing notion that tourists shouldn't visit North Korea because it will only help to support or prop up their government. However, the amount of money the North Korean government makes from tourism is quite insignificant compared to their GDP and other sources of income. As of 2017, approximately 5,000 internationals had visited the country each year, which doesn't equate to a significant amount of money compared to other sources of income. The amount is so insignificant that tourism doesn't even rate in the current analysis of their economy.[3]

People also argue against going to North Korea because of human rights issues. Personally, I am against human rights abuses everywhere, all the time. In my view this is the only position where one can maintain the moral high ground.

The question of detainment of American citizens in North Korea is a difficult one to answer. On the one hand, we who work inside North Korea are keenly aware of the risks involved. Still, we are willing to take them because we see the value of engagement as outweighing the potential downsides. On the other hand, we understand most of the American citizens and others, who have been detained, have actually violated North Korean law in some manner. In the end, it should be recognized that North Korea is not the only country where American citizens or other nationals could be detained. Singling out the country as if it is the only place in the world where visitors might be treated harshly, is not only unfair but fails to recognize the upsides to engagement.

Some people also question whether it's turning a blind eye when visitors to North Korea are treated well, fed plenty of food and lodged in the nicest accommodations while local people are suffering. An analogy might be, isn't this like visiting someone's house where they only show you their game room where they have a big screen TV and an Xbox, they offer you lobster, but in other rooms of the house people are starving and being tortured?

The main problem with these kinds of analogies is they can apply to many different countries in the world, where people would never object to someone visiting. Few would object to people visiting China although they have human rights issues with child labor. It seems hypocritical to me to have such double-standards regarding social justice. People seem to think North Korea is the only country in the world with such issues. The United States has significant human rights issues, yet when talking about North Korea, people tend to completely ignore our own problems. We have two million people incarcerated in one part of the penal system or another. We have many for-profit prisons where the longer a person stays incarcerated, the more money the prison makes.[4] In 2016 over half a million people were homeless in the U.S.[5] We face issues with child sex trafficking, income disparity and a host of other problems, which prevent us from taking the moral high ground when arguing about human rights issues in other countries.

If somebody from another country visits Los Angeles, California, the tour company would never take them to see the local prisons nor would they take visitors to skid row. Instead, they would visit Beverly Hills and Hollywood. They'd eat at nice restaurants, stay at nice hotels, and the tour company would make sure they had the best time possible. If this is the case in the U.S. where we have significant problems, why would it not be the case when visiting North Korea? My point is not to justify traveling to North Korea while ignoring human rights issues. Instead I am simply pointing out if a person complains about human rights issues in North Korea, they should at the very least also be willing to do some navel gazing of their own.

There are three ways in which social justice issues might be improved in North Korea. The first would be to replace their government. This is commonly referred to as "regime change" usually by means of war, but also through an external force of a governmental collapse. If we have learned anything from the invasion of Iraq, it should be that replacing a government is no easy task and the unintended consequences of such an act may often be far worse than the original state of the country.

In addition, a second Korean war would be so horrible; I hate to even contemplate it. When asked about the possibility of a second Korean War, James Mattis put it most succinctly, "A conflict in North Korea would be probably the worst kind of fighting in most people's lifetimes," he said in his first official interview as Secretary of Defense. "The North Korean regime has hundreds of artillery cannons and rocket launchers within range of one of the most densely populated cities on earth, the capital of South Korea." General Mattis also added: "But the bottom line is it would be a catastrophic war if this turns into a combat if we're not able to resolve this situation through diplomatic means."[6]

The second would be to do nothing and hope the situation might somehow improve from within.

The third would be to seek to influence the country and leadership in ways which might cause them to implement reforms of their own accord.[7] This third approach is the best option to influence current social justice issues in North Korea. In no way is it naive to hold this position, in fact, it's the only way in which we can visit the country.

The typical response I get to this idea is to suggest that we, in some way, isolate them more, as if this would somehow magically solve the problem. Ironically, the same people who make this kind of suggestion are the same ones who repeatedly complain that North Korea is the most isolated country in the world. We should not complain about that fact and at the same time hinder those who are doing their best to positively impact the situation.

Complaining about North Korean social justice does not make one a social justice champion. Nor does it make one particularly virtuous if a person complains but does nothing to actually improve the situation of those who they proclaim are oppressed. People who only complain and do not contribute to workable solutions, are a part of the problem.

To those who still think people shouldn't visit North Korea, one might ask, "What better ideas do you have for improving the situation?"

If we are to see improvements in relations between North Korea and the rest of the world, then we need to be focusing on areas where we might see relationships and friendships built. No matter how big or small, fixing the relationship issues between North Korea and the rest of the world is crucial. When we engage North Korea, even if the engagement only produces small positive effects, these are nevertheless steps in the right direction.

You, the reader, might then ask how foreigners entering North Korea can help better the situation. This is a fair question. We might also ask other questions. What are politicians and policy makers on all sides currently doing to bring peace to Korea? Have current policies been effective in improving the situation? Has the policy of "strategic patience" worked? Are we going to wait another 60 plus years on this failed policy?

Ryley Snyder tries on a local man's hat. 2014

Probably the most important question to ask is whether Korea is safer or more dangerous today than it has been in the past? Recent news headlines likely provide the answer. It's quite apparent that politicians and policy makers have taken us down paths of failed policies, and a new way forward needs to be found.

So how then can foreigners help improve the situation? The best answer is that foreigners, whether on tours, engaging in non-government organization (NGO) work, business development or education, provide direct positive impact between local North Koreans and the world. Traveling there not only helps them to open their country, but also to have a better picture of how the outside world looks. Today, North Koreans cannot easily travel outside their country. However, for every foreigner who visits their country bringing their own culture and ideas with them, North Koreans get a better picture of the realities outside their borders.

When we travel to North Korea with an open mind then every wave, every smile, every hand shake, every kid on a surfboard or skateboard, every conversation, every high-five is beneficial in breaking down existing barriers. In their paper entitled "The Role of Tourism in Unifying the Two Koreas," Yong Kwan Kim and John Crompton put it best: "Tourism appears to be a viable way of opening a path to peace by eroding the seemingly invincible wall that has divided Korea."[8]

This is not only the case with tourism to the country but all avenues for engagement. When visiting North Korea, foreigners only get to see pieces of the entire picture, but this picture is constantly changing, often for the better. Visitors might not be able to connect with everyone they see, but they can connect with some. Tour leaders and NGO workers naturally realize what many in government have failed to comprehend, that in order to see improvement in the relationship between North Korea and the rest of the world, there is simply no alternative to engagement.[9]

Whether we accept it or not, whether we support it or not, North Korea is slowly opening. Their messaging seems to be softening. People visiting the North should only be seen as helping this process. In the end, small increments of positive influence can produce very large results. How much of the current positive developments happening inside North Korea can be attributed to tourists visiting and exchanging culture? We may never know, but I suspect foreigners visiting the country have had an immense impact.

To quote Daniel Jasper, "There is no substitute for the firsthand experience and insights that come from regular interaction and communication."[10]

This is why the international community should continue to engage North Korea through tourism as well as through all other avenues.

Useful Idiots?

When people choose to travel to North Korea and engage with its people, they're likely to get labelled as "useful idiots." The term comes from the former Stalinist Soviet Union, where western visitors believed the propaganda of the USSR and supported its system. No doubt some people do agree with the North Korean political system.[11] Indeed, I have met people who completely agree. However, it's a popular misconception that those who visit the country are actually required to fully endorse the system. Of course, the North Koreans may hope visitors would agree with their ideology, although believing in their system is in no way a requirement for visiting the country. In fact, I don't agree with their ideology and have quite different beliefs. As long as I show respect for their government and North Koreans as people, in spite of our differences in ideology, there is no problem in visiting North Korea.

Taking a hard line stance, "You are either with us or against us," and labeling anyone visiting the country as a "useful idiot" is unhelpful. A simple truth is that North Koreans and the international community do not need to agree on everything. Of course there are major problems which need to be solved, however, focusing only on those issues has never improved the situation. Whether you are a politician, diplomat or tourist, focusing on negatives and differences will get you nowhere fast. This is true in every country and North Korea is no different. There are areas where we need to realize that it's okay to agree to disagree so things can move forward.

Traveling to North Korea

How Do I Get There?

People often ask if anyone can go to North Korea. Many seem to think it's impossible to enter the country and it's totally closed. In fact, provided travelers are issued a visa, citizens of most countries can travel to North Korea. There are currently only three countries who have difficulties traveling there. South Koreans are largely blocked from travel to the country as are Israelis and most recently American citizens.[12]

I also get asked if North Korea is a dangerous place. Generally speaking it's probably the safest country you could visit because you're going into North Korea as a visitor on the invitation of the government. The government is the highest respected entity in the country so a local person would never do or say anything offensive to a tourist.

Of course, they do their best to show a good face, especially to tourists. They are very proud of their country and try their best to show us their positive side.

Obviously they don't want guests focusing on negative things, but who would? The worst experience I had in North Korea occurred while traveling on a bus. A group of teenage boys were standing near the roadside and one of the boys flipped me the middle finger. I guess he wanted to show off to his friends or something.

There are various avenues for entering the country. A traditional way to enter North Korea has been through NGO or nonprofit work. This has been a customary way of going into North Korea since the famine era in the 1990s, where people would go under an NGO umbrella to help in areas of great need. NGOs have done amazing work building and helping in hospitals, clinics, kindergartens, preschools, and providing assistance with agriculture and many other projects. These kinds of NGO endeavors have had a major impact on individual lives, and are another great way to engage North Korea from the ground up.

Education is also an avenue where a person can go into North Korea and teach local university students. Pyongyang University of Science and Technology or PUST for short, is the only foreign-run university in the country where teaching staff is comprised of foreigners teaching North Korean students.

The easiest way, and also consequently the most expensive way, is to visit as a tourist. There are different travel companies offering tours to North Korea, such as the one I've worked with in the past called Krahun Co. (pronounced like Crown), which is the only foreign run tour company based inside North Korea.[13] There are also several other travel companies which can be found via an internet search.

Visiting North Korea as a tourist is the easiest way to discover the country. While some people are against anybody traveling to North Korea because they believe the entire experience is somehow set up, they are incorrect in their view. It's true that the capital, Pyongyang, is a showcase city, a sharp contrast to the areas beyond the city limits. It's also true that tours are tightly monitored by tour guides. There are times where certain experiences are set up for tourists, however, the vast majority of any tour is simply seeing life in the country as it is. It would be impossible for every person seen along the way to be part of some grand conspiracy to trick all the tourists.

Unfortunately, North Koreans cannot easily travel outside their country. Hopefully someday they will be able to openly visit us. For now, since the door is open for us to go to them, we should be ready and willing to engage, despite the risks and challenges in so doing.

What is it Like in North Korea?

I often get asked what it's like in North Korea. It's an interesting question. I'm not sure about people's preconceived notions. Maybe they have an image in their minds that may be based on books they've read. Maybe those books came out during the famine era so they think that everybody in North Korea is starving today. Possibly people have some other apocalyptic kind of a view where the entire country is in some sort of collapsed state. Typically the picture people have in their minds is based on what they've heard or seen on the news, which tends to focus only on military or nuclear issues. What is absolutely true is that there is a tremendous amount of misunderstanding about the people and about the problems they face.

Perhaps the best way to describe what it's like in North Korea is to say it's everything you'd expect it to be, and at the same time nothing like you'd expect it to be. There's currently no widespread famine in North Korea, which is of course a very good thing, but a typical visitor isn't going to see any of that anyway. On recent trips, tour guides have been open about the fact that they have problems which they are trying to solve. They've also been open and honest about the fact that many of the issues their country faces are challenging, and that solutions are often difficult to find. What they don't like is when the outside world tries to force change upon them. The North Koreans are not closed to change or dealing with the problems they face. They simply want to deal with their problems and open their country in their own way.

As a visitor, you're not going to get very deep access into the "normal" everyday lives of local people. You are probably not going to be able to hang out with locals in their houses. Even though much has opened, there are still restrictions on those kinds of activities so it's hard to tell what life is like for the average, everyday North Korean behind closed doors.

Stevie Lujan playing his guitar in Kim Il Sung Square. 2016

There are however readily apparent contrasts, which can be clearly seen when visiting. There's a technological contrast with information technology coming into the country and people desiring more material possessions. Today you can see many Chinese-made electronic gadgets inside shopping centers. They also have their own tablet computer, which is not a bad piece of hardware (I have one). At the same time, you have the idea of embracing new technology contrasted with farmers who are by and large planting and harvesting their crops by hand.

There is a contrast between the rich beauty of the untouched mountain regions and the lower mountains which are totally barren of trees. On many of these mountains the trees were cut down for increased farmland and fuel. This has caused problems with flooding that can only be fixed by replanting those trees. These are just a few of the contrasts which I have personally observed in North Korea.

In my experience, North Koreans are very much just like you and me. They're people doing their best to live a good life and take care of their families and see that their kids have a good education and future. There are many beautiful things about the country and the people but not unlike many other countries, there are people in North Korea who have hard lives. Just as it is the case in many places around the world, you'll encounter income disparity, as some people have access to more resources while others have less.

The main difference is their political system which is quite different than the West. When you visit the country, you get the idea that they have a strong veneration for their leaders, specifically Kim Il Sung. This veneration permeates everything in the country.

Photography

Upon arrival in North Korea, after passing immigration and customs, visitors are met by local guides. It's during this first bus or taxi ride that the guides give a list of dos and don'ts. One of the things they talk about is photography. The general rules are visitors can take photos of anything but military, construction (military members are often also construction workers) and close up photos of local people without obtaining their permission first. The last one is kind of common sense as you would not want some stranger pointing a camera at your face and taking your photo without your permission. The guides kindly explain that local people are a bit shy and they'll probably not want to be photographed.

Other than those spoken rules, you would also not want to take photos of what they would consider poor people (this rule is often unspoken). The reason for this should be obvious to anyone who understands the Asian cultural issue of "saving face." In Asian cultures in general and specifically Korean culture, the notion of "saving face" is incredibly important. It is the desire to avoid showing any weakness or failure,[14] and understanding this concept is essential when visiting not only the North but most Asian countries. Taking photos of poor people would necessarily reflect badly on the country and cause them to lose face. Those kinds of photos may be deleted by the military, at the border or possibly by the guides.

Although photos may at times get deleted, in over 10 years of traveling in North Korea, I've noticed that we

Local taking selfie with my daughter Hope. 2013

have much more liberty to take them than ever before. I laugh when I see photo essays on the internet where a person claimed to have brought out illegal pictures of the country. Very rarely have I ever seen photos that were much different from any I have been able to take, and those with the full knowledge of the guides.

More recently, local people have been known to approach visitors and ask them to take photos together. When visiting with my family, locals really wanted to meet our children and take photos with them. As recently as August of 2017, my groups had locals approaching us wanting to take pictures together.

For the most part, in previous years, you could ask, but more often than not they would kindly refuse. People approaching us for photos is something unexpected and new. It might be a small thing, but both the fact we have more freedom to take photos, and local people's desire and openness to do so with us, is an indication things are opening in new ways.

What Not to Do When Visiting

Most foreigners who visit North Korea are unaware that the country has a distinct legal system. It is quite different than in the West. In order to visit, we have to go on their terms, abiding by their laws. Problems arise because as foreigners, we tend to want to visit on our terms and get offended by the fact that we can't. This is what gets people in trouble.

I don't think that people should avoid visiting the country because you have to abide by their terms. One would hope the tour companies and NGOs who take people into the country would adequately brief their travelers about what to do and what not to do. In my briefings, although there are other minor areas, I focus on the following three main areas of the North Korean legal system:

1) If a person enters the country illegally, they will be detained and prosecuted. *Definitely do not enter into North Korea illegally.*

2) As visitors, we need to *be careful to show respect* to the North Korean system of government. As stated above, foreigners don't have to agree with their ideology or their system, but they should in all cases respect the people, even those with whom they might disagree. A visitor would not want to enter North Korea with an adversarial attitude towards their government.

3) *Visitors cannot openly share their own beliefs,* be they political or religious. We've seen in the past, cases where people have tried to promote their religious beliefs that have resulted in their being detained. Leaving Bibles behind or

distributing religious or political literature is not acceptable in North Korea.

Some may say this is reason enough for people not to visit the country. Whether we disagree or agree with their laws, we need to have some sort of presence in order to engage. If we enter the country with basic knowledge of their laws and basic standards of what not to do, then we will find many doors of engagement open and the risks largely mitigated.

Don't They Hate You?

Another question I get asked fairly frequently is whether North Koreans hate me because I'm an American? In their education system, people are taught that America is their enemy, which is reflected in the political animosity they have against the United States. So with that in mind, one might expect that I'd be disliked or even hated there. Interestingly, I've not found this to be the case.

Furthermore, I do not go there with intention to "teach them." Nor do I go with the intention of changing them. Instead I go with the intention of being a "learner" who genuinely desires to understand the people, what they believe and how they live. This kind of position underpins my trips to North Korea and seems to be a really effective approach to engagement. When I go with a heart to understand the people, to engage and love them unconditionally, even those who consider me their enemy respond the opposite way you might think.

This is the attitude I try to have when traveling. Whether in North Korea or the U.S. or in China or elsewhere, my goal is to love and accept people unconditionally. Maybe it's difficult to hate somebody that loves you in this way. Possibly that is why I've never had a North Korean say they hate me.

The Edge of the Box

Since some people have been detained in North Korea, NGOs and tour companies are fairly strict with their guests because they don't want anybody getting into trouble. As I stated previously, there are some things people can't do in the country. We can't criticize their government, pass out religious literature or promote outside religious beliefs. Taking photos is somewhat restricted, and of course illegal entry into the country is strictly prohibited. Other than these main guidelines, visitors have more liberty than they might otherwise think. If a guest ends up violating a rule, which may be related to the others, their guides will inform them. These are usually minor issues, and as long as guests stay within the main rules and cooperate with the guides, it is quite safe to visit the country.

Problems have occurred when guests have violated North Korean laws. This being the case, tour leaders tend to keep their guests far away from the line of breaking any laws, so nobody gets in trouble. If we look at their laws as a box, then many visitors are pushed as far inside, away from the edges as possible.

This is totally understandable, however, since visitors are prevented from venturing towards the edges of the box, they don't really have opportunities to engage with regular people. Consequently, visitors

Stevie teaching kids the hang loose sign in Kim Il Sung Square. 2014.

to the country tend to see local people as cold and standoffish. In my experience, locals aren't unfriendly unless I am. So my conclusion is when foreigners visit North Korea and have to play by the tourist rules, they are the ones who appear nervous, cold and standoffish, which then causes locals to respond in kind. This is my evaluation based on my own experiences and based on observing other groups.

My philosophy is to push people I take to the country out to the edge of the box. Some may call this

Anthony in the mix with local kids. 2016

irresponsible, however, I want my groups to engage with local North Korean people as much as possible. Staying far away from the edges prohibits engagement. Of course I don't want anybody to go outside the box and get in trouble, but I do want them to interact with local people. It is my hope in doing so, that local people will get the feeling that foreigners care about them.

For many local people we meet, this might not be any sort of deep thing. It might only be a wave or a smile at someone on the street, but any kind of engagement is beneficial. It's awesome when my group members find opportunities to high-five local people. Maybe it's a local guy riding a bike down the street in Pyongyang or Wonsan, and someone from my group tries to high-five them. It might be awkward for the guy but more often than not, he tries to give the high-five in return. Even though it's a small thing, it is engagement on a local level. These are the kinds of experiences my groups have.

Engagement doesn't have to happen only in restaurants where the waitresses ask guests to come up and dance. Although that's an amazing thing, there is so much more interaction one can have, if we are okay with pushing out to the edges of the box. As an example, in one instance one of my groups was walking down the street in Pyongyang, when we met a crowd of kids near Kim Il Sung Square. We asked our guides who the kids were and they explained that the group had come from the countryside to the capital city on a field trip. This would be equivalent to an elementary school trip from a rural community in the United States going to Washington, D.C. This was a big deal for them, and as they were seeing Kim Il Sung Square, my group of "big nosed" foreigners walked up. One of our guides said they probably had never seen foreigners before so we began to smile and shake their hands, taking photos and showing them the Hawaiian surfer hang loose sign. It was a brief, but a great moment, hanging out with local kids who had never met foreigners before.

A few years later when we were touring a historical site, we ran into a large group of kids going to a swimming pool. My group didn't stand in front of the kids to take photos. Instead, they got right in the middle of the group of more than a hundred kids. One of my guys took a photo in the middle of the kids with a blow up tube around his head. He was right there engaging and sharing life with the local kids. These are two examples of my philosophy of pushing out towards the edges of the box.

We meet people on the "tourist path," such as the guides, bus drivers, hotel workers and restaurant waitresses. We also meet all sorts of locals along the way in shops and on the beach. Whoever we meet, it's always my hope that they have a good impression of us.

On one trip, I met a local elderly man from the city of Hamhung. He was walking towards me on a path. I went to give him a high-five and he grabbed my hand and wouldn't let go. This made me a bit nervous, but with a big smile, he proceeded to tell me in Korean that he was very glad I had come to visit his country.

Another occasion was during a ping-pong tournament with our local guides. After the tournament was finished and we were getting ready to leave, the woman who took care of the room came in to straighten things up. One of my group members saw an opportunity to bless her so he asked one of our guides to translate for him. He then thanked the woman for taking care of the room and told her what a great time we had, and how much we appreciated how well she does her job. He then picked up a vase of plastic flowers from a table, flowers which belonged to the room she took care of, and then presented them to her. She had likely never had a foreign tourist say something like this to her, and she began to tear up. Why? Because friendship and an expression of thankfulness really touched her heart.

Some of my trips take place during the summer holiday season. There are often hundreds of local people on the beaches we visit. Many are from provincial cities who are out with their work groups. Others may be enjoying a beach day with their families, and their kids see us out surfing and want to give it a shot. How awesome is it for us to be able to have local kids get on surfboards? Even if they never catch a wave, we are able to meet and engage with them in a way which transcends all political barriers.

Today, foreigners can interact with people not only on the tourist path, but also meet and engage with people from all levels of society. This may pose some risk, and fortunately I have not left anyone behind, but it's my experience that when we push out to the edge of the box, we are able to engage local people in

Ryley encouraging a local hotel worker. 2014

amazing ways. Even though it may be limited, we are able to enter into their culture. But the door swings both ways, as they also meet us and encounter our culture. In doing so, we get a glimpse into their lives and they get a glimpse into ours. I believe this is the kind of positive engagement of which no political strategy currently takes advantage. Nonetheless, this kind of positive interaction is possible and I believe has the potential to make a big difference.

Humanitarian Work

Lights in the Darkness

One of the first things you notice at night in North Korea is the absence of light pollution. On clear nights, it's great to be able to see the stars. Unfortunately when it's rainy, visibility is pretty low. Walking out of the hotel restaurant in Rajin one rainy night, it was pitch black and rainy and I happened to step in a puddle of water. Of course my immediate reaction was to be upset about the fact I'd just gotten one of my only pair of shoes totally soaked. My next thought was to wonder why I had not brought a flashlight along to aid me in the darkness. I then thought about those no-battery flashlights you see on TV, the ones with a magnet that you shake through a coil to produce electricity. Finally the thought occurred that if I had I brought one, it could be given away to someone who would then be able to have a light at night.

After returning home, I began to think about this idea of flashlights. How could they be sent to a place where it might be difficult to get batteries? With another trip approaching, I began looking for no-battery lights. Fortunately, I was able to find a hand-cranking flashlight that I took along to show the officials in North Korea. Unfortunately, the timing of my trip was bad, as their leader at the time, Kim Jong Il was experiencing health problems, and my visa was not approved. So I asked a co-worker who was able to go in, to give my flashlight to one of the local leaders and ask if they might want more. She was able to do so and they

Local women receive a hand-crank lantern. 2011

gave me permission to distribute them to local people. Upon returning home, a friend began to help me search Chinese manufacturers for the best type of no-battery light system.

Everyone who heard about the idea got excited. After briefly sharing at a dinner, about a $1,000 U.S. was raised for the project and we were well on our way to funding the first large number of lights to be sent to North Korea. Then as an NGO, we began a one-for-one giving program where if supporters made a donation of $20.00, they would get a lantern to keep and we would send one into North Korea on their behalf.

On one occasion, during a later trip, I was with a group in a restaurant for dinner and the electricity went out. We were in the process of paying the bill and couldn't see anything so someone ran out to the truck and got a lantern. When we put it down on the counter the workers said, "Good, now we can see!" We told them they could keep the light so if the electricity went out again, they would have light.

As of this writing, we've been able to send over 10,000 lanterns all over the country through various channels. We always hear the same thing when we give out the lanterns, "Now we can see!" It's pretty amazing how such a small thing like a light can change people's lives. The irony is this all came about because I stepped in a puddle during my first trip to North Korea.

Driving

That first trip was also interesting because I had the chance to drive while in the country. On our way into Rajin City, our group consisted of a Korean-Chinese driver, and an elderly Korean NGO worker named Dr. Kim who was my host, and two guides from the overseas Korean department. Their department takes care of Korean-run NGOs, and they joined us at the border. We visited several of Dr. Kim's projects inside North Korea, as well as a clinic my church in Hawaii had helped him build.

When we were just about to leave for China, we found out the Korean-Chinese driver had to stay back in the city to take care of some business. The problem was the guides didn't drive. They don't even have licenses because driving in North Korea is a vocation. If you're a driver that's your job, and if you have another job that doesn't require you to drive, there would never be a need for you to have a driver's license.

We were ready to leave for China and were standing in front of the Hotel when I overheard a conversation between Dr. Kim and our guides. They were speaking in Korean, which I understand just enough to get the gist of a conversation. Details often elude me and speaking is not my strong point, but I could understand some of their conversation, especially since they were talking about me. Dr. Kim was saying that we didn't have a driver so I needed to drive us all to the border. Their response was something like, "No way, this guy can't drive. You know this is his first time in the country, and he's an American so he can't drive!" Although Dr. Kim wanted me to drive, he didn't argue the point, and he then drove to Sonbong City. We then stopped off at a soymilk factory with which his NGO was involved.

When we finished visiting the factory, Dr. Kim again explained to the guides that he couldn't drive. Again they said no but he insisted he was not able to do it and if I didn't drive, then we simply could not get to the border. The guides finally agreed but they weren't happy. Dr. Kim handed me the keys and I was thinking, "Okay, I guess I'm driving in North Korea. Awesome!" I was without a driver's license because I had left it back in China but I agreed to drive. I figured it was fine because I had two North Korean guides who were government workers, so if anything happened they would vouch for me.

We all got into the car and the guides were visibly nervous so I started playing it really casual and said, "Don't worry about it, I've been driving since I was 15 and had my own car when I was 16. It'll be fine." That didn't seem to work all that well because then they were really, really nervous. We drove off with the two North Korean guides gripping their seats with white knuckles, terrified because here was this American guy who they've known for all of two days and they are basically putting their lives in his hands. In addition, at that time, the road between China and Sonbong city was a dirt mountain road and it was a rainy, muddy day. Suffice it to say, they weren't having much fun. As for me, I was having a blast!

It was pouring rain and muddy, and about halfway to the border, we had to pass a big Chinese semi-truck. In the middle of the pass, the rear end of the SUV got somewhat out of control. I looked into the rear view mirror to see horror in the eyes of the guides. In my mind it wasn't that bad so I just accelerated out of the skid and made the pass. Strangely though, after the pass, they seemed to be a little relieved. It was as though I proved myself and by the end of the trip, they felt a lot more comfortable with my driving. In fact, when we got to the border one of them commented, "He's a pretty good driver." Since it was my first time in North Korea, driving was not something I ever thought I would be able to do, and certainly not something I've been able to do since. It was an awesome experience nonetheless.

Surfing in North Korea?

The Beach Boys famously sang about surfing, "Catch a wave and you're sitting on top of the world."[15] Birthed from the desire of the ancient Polynesians to ride the waves which pounded their island shores, in the last century, traveling surfers have taken the sport of surfing around the globe. By the turn of the century, surfers had explored virtually every country with a surfable coastline. Every country, except one, which remained totally closed to this ancient sport of kings.

During my first visit to South Korea in 1997, I visited Haeundae Beach where there were some small waves. Having no gear, the only option was to go out for a bodysurf. While catching short rides on those small waves came the realization there was actually surf in Korea, and the coast was probably largely unexplored by surfers, especially in the closed North. This was the day seeds were firmly planted in my mind for further wave riding in Korea. I carried this idea in my mind as I returned to Hawaii and eventually prepared for the move to Korea to do humanitarian aid work in the North.

Sometime in 2006, not too long before making the move, there was a TV news story about North Korea launching a missile somewhere on their east sea coast. What was intriguing to me as a surfer wasn't so much the missile but instead what was behind it. In the background, behind the missile, were really amazing waves. After the news story ran, internet surf blogs began to light up about the fact there were waves in North Korea. It was the last unexplored frontier for surfing, and there was talk about someday people being able to go there and surf. One blogger even fantasized about opening a surf camp right on that surf break.

A website called Arctic Surf even went so far as to publish a guide to surf spots in North Korea.[16] For the next several years, it remained a mystery about how it might be done. Since my family was planning on moving to South Korea, and my intention was to begin doing NGO work in the North, I got to thinking about how this might be possible. With the now firm knowledge there were waves that had never been surfed, my plan was to be, if not the first, among the first to ride waves in the country.

In October 2010, I went on a humanitarian aid trip to North Korea to deliver 10 tons of rice. During the trip, I figured it might be a good idea to scope out the possibilities for surf and began asking the guides questions about surfing, whether they'd ever seen people riding the waves or if foreigners had ever come and done so. Their response was "No, we don't do that here and waves are dangerous why would you even think about it?" Trying to convince them that waves can actually be fun proved to be rather difficult, however, I didn't give up the hope I might catch waves there someday.

The following year, I led a small team to do further humanitarian work. During this particular trip, a typhoon hit the Korean Peninsula. After crossing the border, our bus was detoured to the coast due to road construction, and as soon as we hit the coastline my eyes bulged out of my head. Because of the typhoon, the waves were absolutely unbelievable! With no equipment or even time to go out, I was kind of going crazy, my nose pressed to the bus window looking at all of the amazing waves.

Surf spots were all over the place with beautiful conditions and nobody, I mean nobody surfing. A surfer's dream! Unfortunately, I did not have a camera with a good lens and could not document what I was seeing. It was at that time I decided I was going to do whatever it took to go surfing in the country. The process of seeing that happen was long and many other things happened along the way.

An Unexpected Thank You

That particular humanitarian aid trip was not focused on surfing, but instead on our supplying 10 tons of rice to one of our partner NGOs that also ran a retirement home, where I'd previously helped drill a water well. One of my strategies for NGO work in the country is to support partner organizations who already have a footprint on the ground. Since we rely on donors who support the work, we want to make sure we're making their donations go as far as possible. So instead of building our own footprint, we partner with other organizations, which allows us to not only extend our reach, but more importantly get the best bang for our donor buck.

We'd brought lanterns with us, and we had previously sent medicine for the elderly, and were purchasing heating coal for winter and buying a gas generator to run the water well pump. The people who lived in the retirement home thought it was like heaven on earth because the NGO supplied almost everything they needed.

We were able to purchase the generator locally in Rajin City and went to the retirement home to install it. While a few of our group members were helping install the generator, others were taking the opportunity to visit with some of the people living in the home.

My friend who runs the partner NGO had run into one of the residents in the hall. This particular woman was in her eighties, gray hair and a really cute elderly North Korean grandma. My friend asked how things were going and what she had been doing with her time. The woman answered that she had been going up to the mountain to collect firewood for winter because the TV had suggested people stock up before it got too cold. My friend replied she didn't need to collect wood anymore because the visiting group was supplying heating coal for the entire winter. When she heard this, the woman started crying because she was so happy to not have to go out and search for firewood.

A bit later, my NGO friend was in one of the rooms along with an American man from my group and they were chatting with two other elderly women. The manager of the home was also there and my friend was translating the conversation. As they were chatting, the same woman from earlier walked into the room and pointed towards the American and asked in Korean, "Who's that guy? Is he Russian?" (The Russian border is not too far away and there are a fair number of Russians who visit the area.) My friend replied "No, he's not Russian, he's American." The woman's face grimaced severely and she said, "American? You know I fought against the Americans in the war and they killed so many of our people."

Now, this woman is lovely, and I can't imagine her having fought in the war, but apparently she did. My friend then replied, "I don't disagree with you, but many Americans also died in the war too."

The woman then said, "I guess that's true, I'd never thought of it. Well, why is he here?"

My friend replied, "You know the group visiting today? He's a member and they are bringing the coal for you so you don't have to collect firewood. They've brought rice so you can have food to eat. They also drilled the well and brought a generator, which they're installing right now to provide clean water. They've sent medicine and given us lanterns so there is light at night. His group did all of this for you."

In Korean culture, older people never bow down to younger people. To do so would be a huge cultural no-no. However, after hearing all of this, the woman's face changed, it went from serious to very soft and she did something you'd never expect to happen. She walked over to my group member, who had been sitting there a bit oblivious to the whole conversation. She bowed

A team member and I hanging out with local grandmothers. 2011

down to him and said in Korean, "Thank you very much."

For her to bow to a younger person, especially to an American who is younger than her, should simply not happen in any normal circumstances in Korean culture, let alone in North Korea. But the woman did it. Her whole attitude had changed when she realized he was part of the group who had done so much to make her life better. It was tremendously shocking to me when my friend told me the story. Something happened in the woman's heart because we had gone there to help. This is what we call ground up impact where hearts and lives are touched. This is the kind of impact we can see in North Korea today.

Impact of NGOs and Business

Shortly after the death of Kim Il Sung, North Korea faced a series of natural disasters such as flooding and drought, which then caused a severe famine. The famine officially ended in 2002, but during the mid-to-late 1990s, the situation was dire. There's disagreement regarding how many people died but outside sources estimate up to a million people starved to death.[17]

One unexpected consequence of the famine was that North Korea asked for international aid and began to open its doors. Nonprofit groups and NGOs were then able to go into the country to help with humanitarian aid and relief work. Many large international NGOs took the opportunity to assist with the hopes North Korea might open even more. When this didn't happen and after the famine started to come to a close, many of the large NGOs either pulled out of the country entirely or drastically scaled down their operations. Others were asked by the North Korean government to cease operations. At the same time, many smaller faith based NGOs, were able to continue to operating inside North Korea. They may have had a smaller footprint than the larger organizations, however, they had and continue to have a deep impact, engaging North Korean people on the ground at community levels.

Some of the most successful works inside North Korea have been through these smaller faith based NGOs who have generally not gotten tangled up with politics and instead focused on having a long-term impact.[18] This has allowed for a broader scope of activities in areas outside of Pyongyang, with less impact from political issues, which might otherwise have caused serious problems for NGOs with deep political entanglements.

One of my co-workers worked for an NGO that received the majority of its financial support from government funding, the result was that the particular government that funded operations had a huge say in which projects the NGO engaged. I kidded my friend that "non-government organization" was a misnomer for his organization as all the money came with strings attached to that particular government entity.

Other NGOs have effectively avoided having government strings attached to money by keeping those avenues of funding at arm's length. This has helped keep their organizations truly "non-government." These NGOs may have to operate at smaller scales due to relying on private sources of funding, however, they have the freedom to make their own way, generally free of government interference.[19]

NGOs working at local levels also tend to have a better working relationship with local officials than they may have with those in the capital. This is due to the fact that local leadership has immediate interest in the affairs of people for which they are tasked with providing.[20]

In my experience, working with local officials has been generally positive. There have been several instances where having that good relationship has cleared the way for a project or even cleared up log-jams where projects have been stalled out due to some sort of misunderstanding, bureaucratic issue or lack of permitting. In all of these cases, problems have been solved at the local level by those officials with whom we work directly.

NGOs and even U.N. agencies view most of the positive changes in North Korea as having come from good working relationships that directly benefited local people. This is interesting as NGOs had never operated in the country before 1995.[21] The Rason Economic Zone can be cited as possibly the best example of this concept at work.

This zone is in the far northeast of North Korea and consists of Rajin City, as well as Sonbong City. When it was turned into an international economic development zone in the early 1990s, the "Ra" from Rajin and the "Son" from Sonbong were combined together to make the name "Rason." Unfortunately, not long after becoming a special zone, famine hit North Korea and although there was some local growth, not much happened in regards to large scale economic development.

During the famine, NGO and humanitarian aid work was able to take place in North Korea. Since Rason had already been designated an international zone with fairly easy access to Russia and China, as well as hosting a deep water port, it was a convenient and natural location for NGOs to set up and operate. Probably the most concentrated number of NGOs operating in North Korea are operating in the Rason Economic Zone.

Throughout the famine and into the 2000s, NGOs as well as a few wholly-owned foreign companies continued to work in Rason, helping to raise the standard of living for local people. This rise in living standards didn't happen overnight but through the entire decade of the 2000s.

During my first visit to Rajin in 2007, there really wasn't much going on. It was still pretty quiet as far as economic development was concerned. From my limited observations, there didn't seem to be many people riding bicycles and there were no cell phones. There weren't many cars on the road either. Mostly it was just a few government vehicles and some NGO SUVs, as well as a few Chinese trucks bringing goods from across the border. On my count, there were around eight second-hand Japanese Toyota Corollas and Honda Accords being used as taxis. Before the road was paved, it took about two and a half to three hours to get approximately 50 kilometers from the Tumen River at the border with China to Rajin City. Because the road was pretty rough and they were older cars, the taxis were all fairly run-down.

My next visit to Rajin didn't happen until 2010. I'm not sure what was happening there in 2008 and 2009 but the same NGOs and foreign businesses had continued operating in Rason, as they had been for more than a decade prior. When I returned in 2010, things had really started to develop. Rajin had been made into a special city and had been given a certain amount of autonomy by the central government in Pyongyang.

It was also about this time when Chinese business people started to take interest in the city. Largely due the NGOs and international businesses having been there for 15 years, many local people had reached a standard of living, which made it much easier for Chinese business people to enter the area and set up import/export businesses, construction operations and retail shops.

During a late 2010 visit, instead of eight taxis, I observed there were now 20 older Japanese models. A mere year later during the next visit in 2011, all the Japanese models had been replaced with 30 brand new Chinese-made taxis. There were also a lot more bicycles on the road. While I was walking across the parking lot in the center of the city, a North Korean grandfather crossed my path on a brand new shiny chrome bike. It was possibly the shiniest bike I'd ever seen and his was just one of many new bikes in the city.

Around this time, cell phones also came into Rason as the Egyptian telecom company, Orascom, had built a cellular infrastructure throughout the country. At first, we only saw government workers with phones but that increased as time went by. On subsequent visits, so many people had cell phones, there was not much of a distinction between Rajin and many other cities in the world. In addition to road construction and paving, as well as new streetlights, there were now more taxis, more bicycles and more people around the city.

By 2012, the taxi count had dramatically increased. There happened to be a taxi drivers' meeting during one of my visits, and they were all parked in the center of the city. I asked one of our officials how many taxis there were in the city and he said he thought there were 150. I observed even more widespread cell phone use, more bikes on the road and many more people doing business in the marketplace.

By 2015, which was my last trip to the region, there were three taxi companies. They had closed down the original marketplace, but not for the reasons you might think. They closed it down because it was too small, and with a Chinese construction company the city built a new and much larger market facility in a better area. During the trip, our group was able to drill a well to supply water to the entire marketplace. It was really cool to be there and see the workers put in this well, which would supply clean water to thousands of local people. One of our donors, who had been the first person to support the well drilling project with a $10 thousand donation, was there and able to see the equipment at work. He was able to observe firsthand how his investment in the project was impacting local people in a positive way.

Since my first visit in 2007, the Rason Zone has experienced major economic development. It grew so fast that by 2011 we were hearing rumors of people in the capital wanting to come to Rajin to do business. The market economy in special cities like Rason seems to have been a transformative force, by improving standards of living as well as providing more opportunity for local people. Should we not encourage North Korea to continue down this road of market reforms that bring a benefit to so many people?

Keith with the drilling rig. 2015

In the end, I believe the growth in Rason can be directly traced to the foundation laid by those NGOs and foreign businesses that have been there for many years. What might things look like now, had they not gone into the area and helped people with basic needs? The long term works of NGOs and other efforts that directly benefit average North Koreans through humanitarian aid, education and development should be held up as shining examples of how it is absolutely possible to see beneficial development inside North Korea. It's the low key field workers running these small NGOs and foreign businesses who I believe history will show to have been the real unsung heroes of development in the country.

Micro-Finance

In addition to visiting the retirement home, we also visited the partner NGO's sewing factory in a nearby town. The women who work for this particular sewing factory as their main job are also able to do side work. My friends have set up a micro-finance project where the women have the ability to buy materials from the NGO, make handmade items such as key chains and then sell the product back, which the NGO can use for fundraising. With this system, the NGO is able to train the women in small business principles and it's also a way for them to make money, which they can then use to provide for their families.

When we visited, I ran into one of the women as she pulled up on her brand new pink bicycle. I asked my friend how the woman was able to afford a bike. In North Korea when you get a bicycle, it's the equivalent buying a car in the West. It's a big deal, so I was wondering how she had been able to afford it. My friend explained the woman was doing well with her handmade items and that's how she could afford a new bike.

We've also seen micro-business opportunities where NGOs might provide $250 for a woman to get

Local woman making hand-made items. 2012

set up with a sewing machine and do a small sewing business from home. There are also projects where a local woman might start up a booth in the local marketplace. For about $500, an NGO might assist a woman to get set up with all the licensing as well as all the products, everything she would need to be able to do business in the marketplace.

Other opportunities we've seen, are in farming villages where a set of breeding pigs is provided by an NGO to a family, with the only requirement that the family pay back two pigs from the first litter. These pigs are then used for another micro-finance project either in that initial village or another. Today there are many different ways that we can impact through micro-finance projects and business training development inside North Korea. This is probably one of the best but least known ways for engaging in beneficial development in the country.

Well Drilling

Getting Involved with Clean Water Work

I never intended to drill wells in North Korea. I am not a well driller and have no background in clean water or drilling. The only thing I really knew about water prior to working in North Korea was that when you turn the tap, water comes out.

There is a line from the movie Robots where the inventor robot, Bigweld, says his famous catch phrase, "See a need, fill a need!" What I began to see in North Korea over my time working there was a need for an upgrade in many people's water situations.

During my very first trip to North Korea in 2007, I observed this so clearly while visiting an NGO-run health clinic. My church in Hawaii had donated $20 thousand as seed money for the project and I was the only member to visit. The clinic's water supply, and that of the adjacent village, was a hand-dug well. At that time, the well was basically just a hole in the ground with a cement casing, completely open to the elements. It was also down slope from an outhouse. You can imagine when the rains came what might take place. I remember standing over this well and noticing the water was visibly unclean. This was the main water source that was being used for both the health clinic and an entire village. That moment was the beginning of my really seeing the need.

Many villages in North Korea have hand-dug wells or water supplies that come from streams and rivers. As in other situations in the world such as Africa or Southeast Asia, these water supplies may be contaminated with water-borne bacteria which can cause many kinds of sickness and disease. So when we assist people in addressing this basic need for clean water, their overall health situation can be quickly improved.

While I was on a trip to Rajin in 2010, another NGO worker approached me and asked if I might help to drill a well for the retirement home that his organization had built. Having already seen the need, I agreed and we ended up having a well drilled by the local North Korean-run drilling company in Rajin City. That well was successful on the first try but we found out later that the drilling rig that they use is not able to go through rocks.

We were pretty lucky because when we had them try in other locations, they could not always get water.

They were the only option in town so we continued to have them drill wells, some more successful than others. We'd done about six wells and approached them to drill a few more, but they told us the machine had been moved to another city. We asked when it would be back and they said they didn't know.

We were out of luck, which turned out to be a good thing in the end because the situation forced me to consider whether my organization might be better off purchasing our own well-drilling equipment. If we

NGO worker with local NK drilling rig. 2010

could not necessarily rely on the local company to be available and their rig could not get through rock, then maybe having our own equipment was not such a bad idea.

As I said, I'm not a well driller and have no training whatsoever in this area, but I began to do some research and quickly realized that if this was going to happen, there was no way I could do it by myself. I'd need experts who would be able to not only help in looking at all the factors, but also identifying what kind of machinery to get, but also to train local workers and set up the operation. So I thought we should get our own equipment! It sounded so easy at first.

Having done some initial research, I was dejected. I shared my story of how I believed I needed to get into well drilling with a friend of mine named Bill who was pastoring a church in Seoul. Bill replied, "Hey I think I have a well driller in my congregation." He then introduced me to a retired driller named Dave who had his own drilling company in Montana for 25 years before moving with his wife to Korea to teach at an international school.

I asked Dave if he would like to go to North Korea with me to take a look at the situation and make some recommendations about what I should do. He ended up making several research trips with me and was instrumental in pointing the entire project in the right direction.

It turned out Bill also had a geologist in his church who was also willing to go into North Korea and give his advice. So far so good! A team seemed to be falling into place. The next problem was how to pay for it all?

Have you ever opened your wallet and there wasn't any money there? You kind of open it up and it's like a hollow noise, and you look in and say hello and your wallet echoes back to you, "Hello...hello..." No matter how many experienced people I had in the mix, there was no money in my wallet nor my bank account to purchase well-drilling equipment. However, when things are supposed to happen, there is somehow always a way forward.

I had met a guy named Keith several years before in Korean language school. Neither of us passed the class. In fact, Keith didn't even finish because his Korean girlfriend had broken up with him, and he no longer saw any point in learning her native language. So he just dropped out. I stayed in the class and did my best but after the semester, they told me I hadn't passed. To me this meant I had failed and when I said so, they said "No, no. You just didn't pass." I'm still not quite sure what the difference is, apparently it's a Korean thing.

After dropping the class, Keith visited North Korea on a Diamond Mountain Resort tour that was run by a

South Korean company. People could visit the North from the South but on a very strict tour, only to the resort and nearby mountain. The tour was shut down after a South Korean tourist wandered into a North Korean military camp and was shot. Keith had gone twice, and while there, he began to look for ways he might help. He ended up moving home to the States where he made money in the stock market. We kept in touch and eventually Keith decided to move back to Korea.

Keith verifying a rice delivery. 2011

We met up when he returned to Seoul and I told him about the opportunity for supporting the well drilling. He donated $10 thousand as the seed money to get the project going and also ended up traveling with me on several subsequent trips to North Korea.

In June of 2011, Keith and I, and a Korean American named Ben, traveled to Yanji in North Eastern China. We were supposed to cross the border into North Korea the next day to do a rice distribution project. Ben and I had double-entry China visas and Keith had a multi-entry visa that was good for one year. We needed at least double-entry China visas because once you stamp out of China, that's one visa, and you need the other to stamp back in after visiting North Korea (they don't stamp our passports though). We went across the border only to find the bureau, which was supposed to host us, had somehow mixed up our dates and thought we were coming the following week.

All excited to go into North Korea, Keith, Ben and I crossed the bridge from China only to be turned away. An hour later, we found ourselves crossing back over the river. We were really disappointed and returned to Yanji City. We were pretty sure Keith would be able to go back into North Korea to do the rice project but Ben and I would be stuck in China for the week.

One thing about Keith is he's the kind of guy who needs a lot of time to get ready in the morning. He's not one who just gets out of bed and throws on clothes. No, he needs time, lots of time. Around 6:30 a.m. the next morning my co-worker's niece pounded on our hotel room door. She said Keith needed to be downstairs in five minutes because a taxi was waiting to take him back to the border. Ben and I found it hilarious to watch a guy who needs an hour in the bathroom, struggling to get up and out the door in five minutes. It ended up taking more than five minutes but he made it to the taxi and we sent him off to North Korea.

Ben and I were still stuck in China though, and we didn't really have a back-up plan. I'd previously spent some time in China and had some connections, so I called a friend who was working on an orphanage in another city where we ended up going to help. On the bus ride back, I mentioned to Ben that I didn't know exactly why we were stuck in China but maybe there was a reason. After telling him how I'd been trying to start well drilling in North Korea, I mentioned how I'd met a guy in Seoul about five years earlier named John who was running transportation business inside North Korea. At the time, I somehow felt that someday we'd end up working together but had no idea how.

After arriving back in Yanji, we went to the only American restaurant in town, where I ran into another guy I knew, Mark, who was also doing business inside North Korea. He was part owner in the restaurant and happened to be in China. I told him the story about how I wanted to start a water well-drilling project and asked his opinion. He thought it was a good idea but said at that time, in order to start a new business, the North Korean government was requiring at least a million-dollar investment. Since he knew that wasn't an option, he asked if I'd ever considered a joint venture. I was open to the idea.

He then specifically asked, "Have you ever considered working with John?" I explained that I actually had considered working with John for quite some time and that I'd love to be able to talk to him about it. He also happened to be in China that day but was leaving for North Korea in the morning.

Mark gave John a call and I was able to meet him that evening and spent an hour pitching the idea of well drilling. He said it was really awesome timing because his company that was running buses, as well as an automotive repair service, was already considering well drilling as an expansion of their reach inside North Korea. It sounded like a match made in heaven so we moved forward with the idea of doing a co-venture where my NGO would supply the equipment and experts and his company would provide the business infrastructure and local manpower.

John left China for North Korea the following morning and Ben and I figured out that if we had

gone into North Korea the day before, we would have totally missed him because it would have been almost impossible to meet inside. Keith missed all of this of course since he was in North Korea for the rice project. He arrived back in China, and although Ben still has never made it to North Korea, we were still able to call it a very successful trip.

The following August, I took another group into North Korea. I brought along the geologist from South Africa I had met previously. We were partnering with the same NGO I'd helped to drill the first well at the retirement home. The trip was amazing up until the hosting bureau took us to a village that needed help with their water supply. The water was "brackish" as the village was right on the sea. We met the village manager and it turned out they had previously tried to drill a well with the local drilling rig but couldn't get water. He said their solution was a pipeline from a water source about eight kilometers away, which he estimated would cost a quarter million dollars. When I heard the cost, I regretfully explained that I wouldn't be able to help them because the cost I had in mind was less than $6,000.

Our group returned to the hotel. When I came out of my hotel room for dinner, I heard my Korean co-worker from our partner NGO in a yelling match with the head of the government bureau, and about every other word

Bret, Gabe and local farmer in front of a well house. 2011

I heard seemed to be my name. Even though I didn't pass level one Korean, I understood enough to know something was up so I asked my other Korean American co-worker why they were arguing. She explained they were disputing over the fact that I should have at least offered to assist them and not outright declined to help. Unfortunately, I'd unknowingly insulted the official and damaged my working relationship with his bureau.

Even so, it was a really good trip, and we now had expert geological and equipment recommendations. In addition, when the time came, we had Dave's commitment to train a local well-drilling crew. We also had the avenue for making the project happen through John's company. Keith had put up the initial 10 thousand dollars and with Dave's help, we were able to estimate a start-up cost of $125 to $150 thousand. Although we'd made huge progress, we still had a long way to go.

The next step was to put together a business plan that I could use to present the concept to potential funders. Several business-minded friends helped me put something together and by the end of 2011 we began a fundraising campaign. A friend in Seoul helped me with a video and people started to support the idea as a very practical way of working inside North Korea.

In the spring of 2012, I was invited to Singapore by one of my board members. I was able to raise a major portion of the money needed by showing the video. Several businesses and churches in the U.S. also made large donations. Many individuals also supported, while the rest of the funds came from our church network in South Korea. By the fall of 2012, within 11 months of starting the campaign, we'd raised almost $100 thousand and were well on our way to funding the project. Based on Dave's recommendations and help from John's mechanic, we found a Chinese well-drilling rig manufacturer and began negotiating a deal.

In early October of 2012, a large South Korean church also committed $25 thousand. About that time, John was in Yanji and had emailed me saying we needed to send the final payment to the drill rig manufacturer. It was always nice to get emails from him since they didn't have internet inside North Korea at that time. I'd sometimes have to wait weeks for an answer to an email. Or at best I could send a message to someone in China and they would write it out, hand carry it into North Korea and then bring John's reply back out to China. We called that the "Pony Express" because it surely wasn't efficient. Fortunately, the company later got internet and communication became a whole lot easier.

Since we needed to send the payment, my wife Joy and I headed to the bank to transfer $50 thousand to John. In order to make the transfer, we needed to have everything well documented. It was a Friday afternoon when we went to the bank, the teller on duty informed us that an additional document from the tax office was missing. If we could obtain it by the following Monday morning, she could complete the transfer. I knew this was going to cause John some stress, but there was nothing we could do until after the weekend.

First thing the following Monday, Joy and I went to the tax office, got the proper document and with everything finally in order, headed back to the bank. The bank teller was curious as to why we were sending such a large amount to China. We explained that our NGO was a faith-based organization and that we wanted to assist North Koreans in a practical way by drilling wells. She thought that was nice.

As we proceeded with the transfer, there was a concern in my mind we might not have enough money in our main account to cover everything. A moment later, the teller confirmed this was indeed the case. I turned to Joy to tell her we could move some funds from another account when the woman interrupted to inform us that a large amount of money had just come into our account. The money had literally been deposited right in front of her eyes. The deposit came from the church in the amount of $25 thousand. Not only that but she told us the exchange rate had changed in our favor and with such a large amount, the difference between the previous Friday and right then was almost $5 thousand. It worked out in our favor that we had to wait until Monday.

The transfer went through and John was able to make the final payment, and arranged for the equipment to be shipped to north eastern China and then into North Korea. Dave and I arrived inside North Korea on a snowy day on November 19th, 2012 to receive the equipment that was scheduled to arrive the next day. It was too late in the year and too cold to start work so we were only able to test out the equipment by drilling a hole in the company parking lot. Even though we didn't see any water, it was an exciting first step. In such a short time, we'd gone from concept to seeing all the pieces fall into place. It was a reality. We actually had our own equipment to drill wells inside North Korea. Now the real work had to wait until the following year.

Drilling Wells in North Korea

Dave and I returned again the following summer of 2013. We were able to do a well job for another NGO working in the same area. It was a good test because you never know what glitches you might encounter when using new equipment. And since Dave didn't have any geological work experience in the region, we'd need to try different approaches to see what worked best.

That well certainly tested Dave's abilities, as we experienced equipment failures when drilling through gravel. One of the huge wrenches used to break apart drill pipes cracked and left us with several sections of drill rod still in the hole. We were able to at least get the pipes out by raising the stability jacks on the truck as high as they would go. We got the entire back end of the drill rig off the ground just enough for the drill rod to clear the hole. Our drill bit was stuck on the drill rod, but at least the well was producing water

Dave inspects the new drilling rig. 2012

and we'd learned a lot of lessons. We realized that even though they may look sturdy, tools made in China can easily break. We also realized that we needed additional equipment that would pull well casings down the hole as we drilled through gravel.

We were only able to drill one well that week. I was disappointed we couldn't get more done because it had been a long process and I'd hoped for more success. The fact is everything takes more time to develop in North Korea, and we still didn't have the team of locals for Dave to train.

Something else interesting happened on that trip. On every other trip I'd taken into North Korea, including the previous trips with Dave, I had at least one government guide with me. The guide from the foreign business bureau who had been with us the previous November joined us at the border, and we expected his company for the entire time. After being on a countryside job site one day, we were effectively trusted to do the work without him being present. This policy continued for every additional trip I took for well drilling. My guess is that since we had been there many times and invested so much in the project, we had attained a level of trust we'd previously not been given. If you know anything about North Korea, it's a big deal to go without a guide so it seemed like a good sign we were headed in the right direction.

Not long after that trip, I was able to travel to Houston, Texas to visit Living Water International (LWI). It's one of the largest well-drilling charities in the world. I'd already learned a lot from Dave but this was a great opportunity to go and train with them. In addition, a local church that had donated to the project hosted my family. During our visit, we updated them on how things were going in North Korea.

During the drilling course, LWI staff explained how their work had started in Africa. They'd purchased

Dave drilling the first well. 2013

an expensive rig capable of doing oil exploration and repeatedly sent workers to Africa to drill wells. It took them five years to get a single drop of water out of the ground. Hearing their account, I felt somehow comforted that we'd done ours in Korea in less than half the time. Not that I was happy it took them so long; it just helped me to put things into perspective.

Not many wells were drilled between the first well in 2013 and 2014. Without a crew and a solid block of time for Dave to train them, we were stalled. Things being as they are inside North Korea, we can make plans, but things don't usually happen as fast as we would like. Our priority was to put a plan in place for Dave to spend enough time inside to get things rolling the following spring.

John's transportation company had workers who were interested in learning, and one local worker was hired to be the main well-drilling technician. One thing we determined was in order for Dave to go back to North Korea, his wife Beth would need to join too. We also knew we'd need to have funding in place to help cover their expenses. The next step was to do another fundraiser with the goal of sending Dave and Beth to North Korea to train the crew.

The fundraiser title was catchy: "Help send Dave and Beth to North Korea!" Obviously not something you see every day or even something most people would even consider possible. Thankfully it worked and we raised enough funds to pay for their airfare and ground expenses for both China and North Korea. The plan was that they would spend three months in the summer of 2015 inside doing on the job training with the local crew.

The well drilling company is set up as a for-profit business and does drilling work for other nonprofit organizations, Chinese and Russian business people and at times, local government projects. It's a legitimate wholly foreign owned entity that pays taxes and employs local workers. One of the things we wanted to do when we started was to be able to take a portion of the drilling profits and do village well projects at no cost to the local people.

We already had several jobs and humanitarian wells set up, and the local workers would learn as they went. One of the humanitarian wells was for the same village I had visited in 2011. This was the village that had brackish water, which I'd said I couldn't help. When we met the manager, I mentioned I'd been there in 2011. Although he didn't remember, I remembered him and apologized for not helping before. We now had equipment we believed would be able to drill deep enough to get good water. I promised if he could get permission for us to come back the following summer, we'd drill a well. It turns out many foreigners had promised to help and not come through, so he was naturally skeptical. I explained that this was my second visit to his village and if I wasn't serious, I would never have come back. He said he'd work on getting permission and let us know the following spring.

We were also able to visit another village that trip. Each village has a manager who is in charge of whatever that particular village produces. The manager wasn't there at the time but his assistant was. He took us to a location where they thought we could drill a well. While a group of us were walking through a village, a couple local women saw us and asked the assistant manager why the Russians were in their village. Since we'd been drilling the well down the road and the Russian border was not all that far away, apparently everyone thought we were Russian. The assistant manager explained that we weren't Russian but American. The two women were visibly shocked, but he told them we were going to come back the following year and drill a well. They seemed thrilled to hear this and we continued on our way.

That following summer we managed to send Dave and Beth to North Korea for three months to get the project moving. Both villages were able to obtain permission for the company to drill wells. Dave was able to return to one of the villages, but then the hammer came down and they said no foreigners were allowed. The company had done several other jobs prior to this project where they got the drilling basics down, however, this was the first real test for the crew to go it alone. Working inside North Korea is not always predictable and sometimes we just have to make due.

Workers in North Korea are like what you'd expect from construction workers anywhere else. They are rough guys who smoke, drink and swear, everything you'd imagine they'd do. When they first arrived on the well-drilling crew, they considered it a job and

Local boys enjoy water from their new village well. 2014

didn't really see the value of the work. They definitely understand that working for a foreign-owned company is a good position to have but in the end it was still just a job.

So here the guys are in the village without Dave's expertise when a local grandmother walked up. She had been collecting firewood and set down her load and began to weep. One of the workers asked her why she was crying. She replied, "I've lived in this village my whole life and this is the first time we're going to have this kind of access to clean water." Now, you wouldn't imagine this would happen but, as she was crying, these tough construction worker guys cried along with her. Why? Because they suddenly recognized how their work was going to improve her life.

We only know this story because the crew came back and told my co-workers about it. The reason they shared was because they had seen the value of the work in a new way. When they go out into these villages, they are providing such practical and necessary help for their own people. In other words, the job turned out to be more than they had expected. Today, drilling wells in the villages account for their favorite experiences. It has been really encouraging to see this method of bottom up engagement touching lives on the ground in North Korea. Both sides benefit, the people who have their water upgraded and the workers who can be part of seeing people's lives improved.

Things were moving forward. Jobs for NGOs were coming and we had several other humanitarian well projects set up. Everything was going smoothly, until it wasn't. In order for the team to drill a well, the customer has to get five different stamps from five different bureaus. Sadly, one of the bureaus stopped stamping, which caused our work to come to a screeching halt. That bureau just happened to be the same one I'd had a falling out with earlier over refusing to help with the village project.

So, I planned a trip inside to see if there might be anything I could do. My co-workers were able to schedule a meeting with the head of the bureau, who happened to be the same man I'd offended in 2011. He remembered me, and I explained how the company had returned to the village and drilled them a well. In fact, two wells had been drilled, one for their kindergarten and one for the village. I also explained how we were able to help the other nearby village upgrade their water supply too.

I've learned to use the term "upgrade" in North Korea as it has a positive connotation. Who doesn't want an upgrade, right? Upgrade to Business Class? Of course! Putting water projects in positive terms like offering to "upgrade the water supply" helps open doors where they may be closed otherwise. It's amazing what you can accomplish when you choose the right terminology.

In both villages, the company had drilled wells at no cost to the people, something I had wanted to do all along. I'd just not been able to do it in 2011. The bureau chief seemed to appreciate the heart behind what the company and I wanted to do so I asked if he could work with us by sending the company to villages that needed an upgrade to their water supply. We'd do these wells at no cost as a service and a way of giving back to the community. He agreed to do so and from then on things seem to run smoothly when it came to clients getting permission for us to do wells.

Drilling wells inside North Korea has been a very interesting adventure. From having nothing, to seeing the team and money fall into place, to seeing the equipment now living inside the country. Every year has its challenges, but so far we've been able to see 40 wells drilled, some as paying jobs and many others as humanitarian wells for villages, hospitals, clinics, orphanages and schools.

Even though the story is still unfolding, it really came full circle when the crew went to that same village I'd visited in 2007 and drilled a new well. They still have access to the old hand-dug well but now their drinking water comes from a much better source. In addition to those villagers, many thousands of other locals inside North Korea have been impacted by clean water through this work. It all started with my looking into that hand-dug well, seeing the need and wondering what I might do to fill it.

Engagement Through Tourism

Water Filters and Waves

Until recently, the coasts of North Korea remained a mystery to surfers. The closest surfers could get was to pour over satellite imagery and hope someday the country would open up so they could actually go and see the potential for wave riding. Unbeknownst to many, in the 2000s North Korea began opening up to tourists. Prior to that time, most tourism had been from Russia, former Soviet Bloc countries, China and few ethnic Koreans visiting the country from overseas. With this new opening, the opportunity eventually presented itself for surfers to travel to and even surf in this last country on the planet to receive the sport.

I wanted to catch waves in North Korea, but also wanted to figure out how to benefit local people at the same time. Since already being involved in well drilling, I really wanted to find a way to address clean water needs where drilling was not possible. So I begin to think about connecting clean water and surfing. The idea was, if we could assist people with basic clean water needs, it would help us to have a better relationship with the North Korean people and government. Through this improved relationship we might be able to have a more successful time going surfing.

Rob Machado is a well-known ex-professional surfer and former world champion. He had put out a movie called The Drifter in which he helped a village in Indonesia with a water well. Having seen this movie and wanting to connect surfing and clean water, I checked out his website. There was a link on his site to an organization called Waves for Water, a non-profit run by another ex-professional surfer named Jon Rose. Since Waves for Water or W4W was run by surfers doing clean water work, it looked like it might be a good match for a surfing trip to North Korea. So I emailed Jon Rose with the idea of doing water filter distribution and hopefully do some surfing. Jon and his crew were initially skeptical but ended up jumping onboard with the idea.

After about four months of organizing the tour, we landed in Pyongyang in October of 2012. To my knowledge, this was the first ever tour where people actually went with the intention of exploring the coastline for surf. During the trip, we checked out surf possibilities at three locations, Sijung beach, Wonsan Bay and Majon Beach near Hamhung city. Our first stop was Sijung beach on the east coast, which turned out to have really small waves. Still, one of our group members, a woman named Elizabeth took my bodyboard out and jumped into a few tiny mushy waves. She may very well be the first person ever to ride a bodyboard in the country.

A Short Walk

The hotel in Sijung is right on a lake and about a half a mile away from the beach. The man who was leading our group asked our local guide if we could walk from the beach to the hotel. This isn't a common occurrence in North Korea because we usually travel by bus, and it's locals who we see walking. Amazingly, our guide agreed and we started to walk to the hotel along the main road that runs along the coast.

They have military trucks in North Korea that run by burning wood. There's a hopper in the back where they put the wood. Then through a process, it creates a gas that powers the truck. We aren't permitted to take photos of them because they are military and usually have soldiers in the back. When the trucks are loaded, they tend to travel at low speed.

We were walking down the road along the coastline and saw one of these trucks coming towards us. It was traveling around 80 km (50 mph) an hour. As it got closer, we could see a couple men standing in the back against the cab. They looked like they were having a great time and so we cheered out to them while pumping our fists in the air. Just as we had, they started cheering back at us and pumping their fists in the air. It seemed like a bizarre situation to be in North Korea walking on the road like locals cheering at the military guys and enjoying ourselves. I'm pretty sure that was an atypical North Korean experience.

We left Sijung the next day to distribute water filters at a local village near the provincial city of

Jon demonstrates water filters. 2012

Wonsan. On the way to Wonsan we passed a small cove where there looked to be really nice, rideable waves. One of the W4W guys, Christian, asked if we could stop the bus and surf, but we were informed the beach was controlled by the military and no tourists were allowed. After distributing water filters at the village, we continued to Wonsan for lunch and to check out the surf which was unfortunately totally flat.

The following day, we continued up the coast to the city of Hamhung and then stayed at the Tourist Hotel Villas at Majon beach. We had two photographers with us who upon our arrival went down to the end of the beach. One of the rules in North Korea on tours is that you are not to go anywhere without your local tour guides. Not only had the guys gone down to the end of the beach, but they continued along the rocks another 20 to 30 yards where they found some sort of a cave where they started taking pictures.

I knew they'd walked beyond the limits and could see an armed local military guard who was up on the hill above the cave coming down. He went directly to the cave to check on what the foreigners were doing. According to the guys, he was actually really nice but made them delete their photos because apparently it was a "military" cave. The guides ended up telling us the rocks were out of bounds and the photos got deleted. Thankfully everything was fine.

There were no waves when we arrived but overnight they came up and in the morning they were breaking with about three-foot faces. Like a fool, thinking it was going to be flat, I'd left my gear bag under the bus. Listening to the waves all night, it was my hope to track down the bus driver at first light to get my bag. Unfortunately, I had no idea where he was. After breakfast, we had to leave for another village water filter distribution so I never got my bag out and missed catching any waves. By the time we returned in the early afternoon, the surf had again gone completely flat.

Even though there were no waves, one of our guides, Mr. Park, wanted to get in the water to at least get the feeling of paddling a surfboard. Jon Rose had his board and a wetsuit and Christian from W4W gave Mr. Park some basic instruction, and he became the first North Korean to at least paddle a surfboard around. It's a pretty big thing to be the first at anything in the country, and even though he'd only been paddling, he unofficially became known as North Korea's first surfer. A few years later, Mr. Park would officially become the first surfer.

Unfortunately, we did not end up catching any waves on that trip. On a positive note, W4W distributed 45 water filtration systems in two villages.[22] So even though the waves didn't cooperate, it was still a very successful visit. Overall we found the surf possibilities

Christian gives Mr. Park paddling instructions. 2012

to be very limited because there were only a few beaches open to tourists. To this date, it continues to be a place where the traveling surfers will not be able to drive around freely exploring for waves. Hopefully sometime in the near future, this will change as the country becomes more open. It would be a good thing as their coast is in much more pristine condition than that of the neighboring South, where there seems to be a boat harbor on every beach.

Mr. Park paddling on a surfboard. 2012

A *Family Affair*

After failing to catch waves with the 2012 tour with Waves for Water group, my dream of surfing in North Korea had pretty much died. I'd given up on the idea as the beach situation was so limited, as well as the fact you'd have to be extremely lucky to see rideable waves while in country.

Aside from the well drilling trips in 2013, I traveled to North Korea on a tour with my family, an investor in our well drilling work named Keith, a team member named So Young, and some friends. My family consists of my wife, who is originally from South Korea, our three daughters, and myself an American Caucasian man. Because it's rare for bi-cultural families to travel to North Korea, I anticipated that my daughters, Danielle, Charity and Hope, might capture some attention. In fact, we were told by some of the people we met that they had never seen a family like ours. I believe what made that trip so unique was having our children with us. My previous experiences traveling in the country without my family also serve to confirm this view.

While at the Beijing airport, we happened to run into the North Korean women's soccer team. We were all in the immigration line and they were traveling back home to Pyongyang from a soccer tournament. The soccer players were naturally curious about my girls and began trying to guess who their father was (there were several other Caucasian men in the line). Some of the players overheard that my kids spoke Korean and started chatting about how we'd be on the same plane to Pyongyang.

When we boarded the Air Koryo flight, we were in the middle section, toward the front of the plane. The soccer team took up the entire rear section. My older two girls, Danielle and Charity, were across the aisle making a video called "Barbie and Ryan tour to the DPRK," which you can find on YouTube.[23] Our third daughter, Hope, was with my wife and myself.

While Hope got up to help her sisters with the video, a family who was in the next row up from Danielle and Charity, noticed her and the father began asking her in English about our trip. They were a North Korean family, that I gathered were likely fairly affluent, as they had been traveling to different countries. They also had a daughter around the same age as Hope. When the father realized she spoke Korean, he and his wife began asking her all sorts of questions.

I was watching closely as I didn't know who he was. I wondered if he was a security agent and what kind questions was he asking her. He then put her on his lap. Not surprisingly I got nervous. Danielle and Charity were in the next row back listening to the questions he was asking and were also feeling a little uneasy. In general,

Korean people are very friendly towards kids and I'm used to it but I suggested my wife check it out. She went over and met the family.

It turned out they were curious about her and were only asking the standard questions adults ask kids, her age, where she was from and the like. When they heard she spoke Korean, they were even more intrigued and told her she could come to live with them. Joy and I felt badly for their daughter, who was sitting in the window seat, looking somewhat dejected as her parent's paid

The women's soccer team arrives in Pyongyang. 2013

attention to our daughter. Finally, we were able to go back to our seats for landing.

As we got off the plane, the soccer team was behind us. It seemed they were returning heroes for having won their soccer tournament. The local news media was there and the team was marched off to the sounds of a marching band.

While we were waiting for our luggage, So Young took Hope to find a luggage cart. The airport staff heard Hope speaking Korean and swarmed around her like she was the biggest star in the country. Suffice it to say this was only a taste of what was to come on the rest of our trip. It seemed everyone we met totally loved our kids.

After receiving our baggage and passing through immigration, we met our tour guides and boarded a big green Korea International Travel Company (KITC) bus. The bus was made in China and fairly new, and aside from our two tour guides and the driver, we were the only people on board. This remained the case throughout our trip to the DPRK, as tour busses are not allowed to pick up local passengers.

We passed through Pyongyang on the way to a hotel near Nampo City, which is the main port city in North Korea. If you look on a map, Nampo is southwest of the capital and from the airport, it took about an hour and a half to get there. Along the way, we saw many people walking or riding bicycles on the roadside. Our guides informed us that outside the capital of Pyongyang, bicycles are the main form of transportation. There were many people riding bikes but as many or more were walking.

We wanted to be as friendly as possible to everyone we saw and waved from our bus. Many people, including several children, waved back. We were not sure if the locals had been instructed to wave at the big green tour buses passing by or if they were genuinely waving. I have the feeling it was authentic.

When you travel inside North Korea, you get the idea that the people are actually very pleased you are visiting their country. The general feeling people seem to have is that their country is severely misunderstood by the majority of the world. Regardless of the causes of misunderstandings, the feeling appears to be genuine. So when foreigners visit, people seem to be authentically happy to see them. It seems that they're hoping visitors will leave the country with an understanding of their political system and generally good feelings they'll share with others. In turn, this might contribute to a better perception of their county by the rest of the world. Of course this is merely the impression I get during my trips and not a statement of fact.

The hotel where we stayed is set on beautiful grounds and is known for its hot springs that are said to promote health, as well as healing of chronic illnesses. Each room has a   hot tub, and we were encouraged to spend as much time as possible using the private spa that is generally only used by tourists and wealthy individuals. We arrived just as hundreds of white heron birds were settling on the pine trees around the grounds. It was a sight to behold and our tour guides said we were very lucky to have seen it.

As we were walking from our rooms to the main building to have dinner, my wife mentioned that

White heron cranes in Nampo. 2013

our guides had encouraged her to have a clam BBQ afterwards. The clams are cooked using a local super high proof alcoholic beverage that they call "petrol BBQ." This was a little confusing but we finally figured out they were not using gasoline.

We got the feeling that the guides wanted us to partake so they could join in. Only a couple of our team members were interested in trying it so we paid for five servings, including our guides and driver, and they said it would be ready after dinner. When we arrived back

Our group enjoys North Korean-style petrol BBQ. 2013

at our rooms, we found that the bus driver had already set everything up and was waiting for us to come back so he could start. It turned out that he was the one who really wanted to have clams as only this particular hotel offered them. He said that some other groups he'd driven hadn't wanted to try it and he'd been really disappointed. So all in all, we were happy to provide him with some clams to BBQ.

By this time, it was getting quite dark and the driver got out a large battery-powered flashlight. We

Singing around the BBQ. 2013

had brought 20 hand-crank lanterns to give away so this was a great opportunity to hand one out. As the driver was preparing, I went to the room and brought out a lantern to give him. He was pleased and one of our team members said that after the BBQ was finished, he saw the driver walking down the path holding the lantern instead of his big battery-powered flashlight.

Back to the clams, unfortunately, I suffer from a shellfish allergy so I couldn't partake but I did get a chance to observe the process of cooking clams with alcohol. The recipe involves buying lots of clams, placing them in a circular fashion on a stone BBQ, soaking them with the high proof alcoholic beverage, lighting them on fire, adding more alcohol as needed, until the clams are cooked. This seemed to take two bottles of the alcoholic beverage.

The last step is to sit down around the BBQ and eat the clams. This part of the experience is what I believe traveling in North Korea is all about. Our group was able to share an intimate mealtime with our tour guides and driver. I imagine most journalists would enjoy writing about that experience.

One of our members named Daniel had his guitalele instrument with him; it's a cross between a guitar and a ukulele. He pulled out a songbook to play some tunes. It was difficult for him to see so one of our guides offered to hold the songbook as Daniel played. All the songs were Swiss Christian songs so he translated their meaning to us. I realized then how few people get the opportunity to sit down with North Koreans around a fire and share their lives with them.

On our first full day in North Korea, after a European-style breakfast, we set out from our hotel towards the city of Kaesong. We were encouraged by our guides to leave on time because we needed to pass the West Sea Barrage before 10:30 a.m. Constructed to control the West Sea tidal effects on the Daedong River, it is effectively a man-made barrier that allows the river to flow out and keeps the tide from coming in.

We arrived at a lighthouse guest center at the Barrage around 10:15 a.m. and were greeted by the local guide dressed in the traditional Korean hanbok. She ushered our group into a room where we were seated to watch a video of the construction process on a slick, new Chinese-made flat screen TV.

The video was in essence a man versus nature story. There was plenty of footage of stormy seas, men fighting the elements, tons of rock and dirt being dumped into the water and the odd explosion or two. In the end, through blood, sweat, ingenuity and perseverance, man prevails against nature and the West Sea Barrage was born. Evidently, they are very proud of it.

After taking pictures, we left just before 10:30 a.m. as we needed to cross the bridge before the revolving road, a mechanism that allows ships in the locks to pass either into or out of the river, was turned aside. Based on what our tour guides had told us earlier, we expected to see hundreds of ships waiting. While there were fewer than we expected, there were still some ships already waiting in the locks with a few dozen others anchored and waiting. As we crossed, I remember having the hope that sometime in the future, there would be many more ships.

Trader or Traitor?

One of our stops was a hundred-year-old hotel in the city of Kaesong. In spite of its age, the hotel turned out to be quite comfortable. We had a great time in the main room, with its cozy furnishings. It allowed us a place to meet as a group, relax and play card games. I should point out that even though we invited them, our guides never joined us in our meetings.

After checking into the hotel, our guides asked if we would like to walk around the city. I'm not sure if foreigners typically get to walk through Kaesong. I'd never heard of it being possible and I don't hear many stories of other people getting to do it. Here we were, our guides, my family, Keith (wearing a shirt plastered with AMEN across the front) and the rest of our group all walking down the sidewalk in Kaesong, North Korea.

Since my wife was Korean-born and is proficient at languages and accents, she was chatting with one of our guides as we walked. As she was speaking with the guide, I was walking in front of them. I wasn't sure if it was my wife speaking at first. When I turned around and saw her, I noticed she'd unconsciously picked up the Pyongyang accent. She almost fooled me because she sounded so much like the local women from Pyongyang.

After walking around for a while, we visited a famous gate from the old city called the South Gate. This gate dates back to the time when Kaesong was a

The South Gate in Kaesong. 2013

fortress city and once the capital of Korea during the Koryo Dynasty. We were able to walk up to the top, which is about two stories high. It's above the traffic and people began to take notice there was a group of foreigners and would do a double take as they passed by. Probably not something they see every day.

After the gate, we walked a bit more to a hill in the center of the city where the Kim Il Sung monument is situated. There's a nice park on the hilltop where we stopped to rest and talk. Somehow we got on the subject of TV and Keith tried to explain to one of our guides that he has a 72-inch 3D television. He was trying to explain how the 3D glasses worked, animatedly trying to give her some idea of the size. She had never heard of such a thing, although she seemed to be interested in someday seeing what a 72-inch 3D TV looked like.

As we were walking down the hill, our other guide asked Keith about his job. He told her that he doesn't work and she wanted to know how it was possible. He explained how he made a lot of money in the stock market and that now he doesn't have to work. Instead, he now serves as a volunteer in a church, helps people and even invested in our well-drilling project in Rajin.

He began to explain the stock market, how parts of company can be bought and sold and how if a person buys part of a company and that company does well, the value of stock goes up and you can then sell it for a profit. This was all very shocking to the guide and she then asked what his position was. He replied that he was a "trader" which the way he said it sounded like "traitor." She said, "You are a traitor?" Keith hadn't caught the difference in the pronunciation and confirmed that's what he had said.

Fortunately, I had been listening in on the conversation so I clarified the difference between the two meanings. Our guide was visibly relieved. She also learned a lot about the stock market.

As we were walking back down the hill towards the hotel, there was a group of local elderly women hanging out on a bench. They were looking at my daughters and said hello to Hope in Korean. At this point, Hope had her hair dyed bright red for a TV show she'd been on, so she really stood out. As she replied in Korean, they realized she spoke their language and really wanted to take a photo with her. In all my prior trips to the country, I had never experienced locals asking to take photos with foreigners so it was definitely unusual. One woman pulled out a digital camera and then they took photos with my daughter. Everywhere you go in the world, you realize that people are just people and these elderly North Koreans just wanted to capture a souvenir of a sweet little girl.

A *Shocking Experience*

In the hotel, they have a Korean restaurant called "panchan." All of the food is basically side dishes with no standard main course. The seating is traditional Korean style, on the floor. The floor in the restaurant room where we were seated was heated by a modern electrical system.

Hope was sitting next to one of our group members named Iris, and while they tasted each other's food, they somehow touched hands. As they touched, they got an electric shock. It wasn't a normal, small static electric shock, instead it was more like something like you'd feel if electricity was passing through your body. They thought it was strange and tried it again and found it was repeatable. If they touched each other's fingers, the same thing would happen but eventually it would hurt too much and they'd have to break contact. They did some more "tests" with Hope moving to another area of the floor and found it only happened in that one spot.

We all began to try it. If you held onto the other person's hand or finger in that one spot, eventually it would get the point where it would be too much and you would need to let go. We were experimenting, switching positions and holding on each other's hands, getting shocked and having a great time. I don't know about the science of it and it may have actually been super dangerous. Apparently there was electricity leaking out of the floor heating system into the person's body who was sitting in that exact spot. Dangerous or not, nobody was getting injured and we were having a great time shocking each other.

As we were doing all of this, our waitresses kept walking in and out of the room collecting plates. It seemed like they were wondering what the tourists were doing but couldn't figure it out. Finally, I called one of the waitresses over to try it. She touched the end of her

Playing the electrocution game in Kaesong. 2013

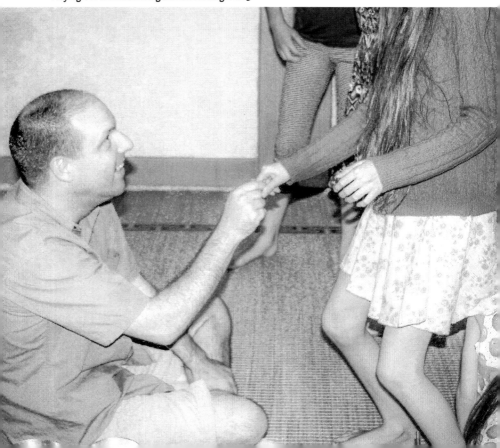

finger to mine and began to get shocked. Terrified, she pulled her finger away and ran out of the room.

After dinner, we continued to play the "electrocute each other" game for some time before a tour guide from another group showed up. We gathered our waitress had been really concerned and told him what was going on. Of course in order to show what was happening, we had to electrocute him too. He didn't seem to like the idea all that much so to our dismay the electrocution game abruptly ended.

A while later, our guides knocked on our hotel room door to make sure we were alright because they'd heard there was some electrical problem in the restaurant. We reassured them and wished they would have been there to enjoy the fun. They seemed to think we were sort of crazy (they might have been correct) and were very concerned. I explained what had happened-that it wasn't a big deal and not to worry.

The next morning, we went to the same restaurant to eat breakfast and could no longer shock each other. I guess in order to make sure everyone was safe, they'd disconnected the power to the floor heating system. Of course, we were a little disappointed we no longer had superpowers.

Breaking Down Walls

A Day at the Border

We checked out of the hotel and proceeded to a local historical museum. One thing I really enjoy about traveling to any country is learning their history. North Korea has actually done a good job of preserving historical artifacts, sites and documentary information. I'm sure that someday all Koreans will be appreciative of the work they have done to preserve Korean history.

Joy spent time talking to the local museum guide who was born and raised in Kaesong. The woman was enthralled with our girls. She'd met foreigners married to Koreans before but never seen a family with three daughters. Apparently, to her knowledge, we were the first bi-cultural family with three girls to ever visit the museum. She also commented on how well behaved the girls were. Joy was able to share how our values have contributed to how we've raised them. It was one of those moments where our presence in the country impacted an individual in a positive way.

After the museum, we visited the stamp shop that's right next door. The shop had numerous stamps but was really just one of the many souvenir shops visitors encounter along the way. Actually there is at least one souvenir shop at every tour stop, so if you ever visit, be ready to buy lots of knick-knacks.

I bought some ginseng candy since Kaesong is famous for its ginseng production. An interesting thing about traveling in North Korea is you can use multiple currencies. Euro, American dollars and Chinese yuan are the most prevalent and you can even pay in combinations of the three. The shopkeepers have calculators handy and know the current exchange rates. It's also likely you'll receive combinations of currency back as change. If they don't happen to have correct change, they might ask you to take another product instead. When I bought the ginseng candy, the saleswoman didn't have change and asked me to take two packs. I didn't really want two packs of candy but obliged her as a courtesy.

Actually what happened in front of the shop was more interesting to me than what was inside. After Hope looked at some stamps, she went out the front doors to sit on the stairs. Our bus driver, as well as three other bus drivers who were his co-workers, were all hanging out on the steps waiting for their groups to finish. Our driver had absolutely fallen in love with Hope. He told us that he'd never seen such a happy child ever! It also turned out that all the other drivers were jealous of him because he was driving our group. So when Hope went outside, she was kindly mobbed by the drivers. She handled it well and spent a few minutes meeting and chatting with them. It was a remarkable scene for me to step back and watch my daughter bring such joy and happiness to a group of tour bus drivers in North Korea.

Our next stop was Panmunjom. Although soldiers face each other all along the border, each is a fair

Hanging out with bus drivers in Kaesong. 2013

distance apart since the Korean DMZ itself is in some places 3 kilometers wide. However, at Panmunjom, both sides are literally facing off directly across the line separating North from South. When tensions are high, this is the place where you see photos of soldiers from the North and South standing nose to nose.

Our group joined three other groups for the Panmunjom tour. The North Korean local guide was a military officer who presented us with their side of the story. Without going into details, their version of

My family with the local guide at the DMZ. 2013

events, both of how the Korean War started as well as how the fighting stopped, is a bit different than ours.

After seeing the building where the 1953 armistice was signed, we then went to the area where both sides face each other. The North has a building overlooking the area. On the other side of the line is the South's equivalent building that has all sorts of high tech cameras facing northwards. It's not far, maybe about the size of a football field away, and we could see the flashes going off. We assumed that our photos were being taken by the Joint Security Forces in the South so we waved as they clicked away. We were then allowed to take our own photos.

One thing you immediately realize when you visit Panmunjom, from either side, is just how close you actually are to Seoul. From Seoul, it takes literally one hour by car to get to the DMZ. It would take 15 minutes to get to Paju City from Panmunjom and maybe 25 to 30 minutes to the City of Ilsan. People in Seoul seem to think that the North is very far away, in fact, it's really close.

Towards the end of our tour, the military guide surprised us by allowing the groups to take photos with the soldiers. Since he had ridden into the area on our tour bus, we wanted to have some photos with him. He obliged and even held Hope for the photo but was rather stoic and serious. We encouraged him to smile but the best we could get was a smirk. I guess he has a serious job and not much cause to smile. Hopefully we can meet again under different circumstances. Until then, we continue to hope and pray for permanent and lasting peace to come to the Korean Peninsula.

Pyongyang

The next day, we returned to Pyongyang where we visited Mansu Hill. This is the hill where they have the two statues of their leaders. After seeing the statues, we ran into the women's soccer team we'd met at the airport in Beijing. They recognized us and greeted us, waving and shouting. We felt slightly awkward as all these local women were waving at us.

Our guides then took us to the People's Grand Study Palace, overlooking Kim Il Sung Square. As you walk into the building, there is a room with a huge statue of Kim Il Sung sitting in a chair. Charity and Hope began to run over to the statue but were quickly stopped by our guides and instructed to walk carefully through the room. Only reverence is allowed in the presence of a statue of their Great Leader, Kim Il Sung.

We met our local guide for the tour of the palace. He was also a manager for the facility and really knew the ins and outs of the place. It's quite a large building. To see it all would have taken more time than we had so he took us to a few points of interest.

Life inside North Korea is governed by the concept of "us." South Korea is still much the same with the idea that the group always trumps the individual. This even shows up in Korean language where the word used for the family or group is not "my" but "our." So "my house" becomes "our house." Rather amusingly, "my wife" becomes "our wife" and so on. It's not that there is no word in Korean for "my" but it is the group that is more important than the individual so "our" always comes first. This concept is really prevalent in the North where the Communist ideology has influenced every facet of society.

Our guide showed us the library where students can borrow from a vast selection of titles. I was curious about what happens when a book is returned late so I asked the guide about their policy. He said that if a student returns a book late there is no individual penalty. Instead their entire class is penalized for the one student's late return. The idea being that the rest of the class will make sure the guilty person never makes the same mistake twice.

He then asked me how it works where I live. I said that it was an interesting question as my oldest daughter had returned a book late to the library just a few weeks prior to our visit. I explained that there was no corporate penalty but that instead, for the amount of days the book was late, that amount was multiplied by four and that was the period of time she could not check out books. He asked if I thought it was an effective policy, to which I replied since my daughter loves to read and she was effectively cut off from borrowing books for a significant period of time, it caused her such unease that she never wanted to return a book late again. So in fact, I believed it was an effective policy. He pondered this for a moment and finally commented that it did indeed seem like an effective approach.

Our group visited a room to observe an English class in progress. The class was quite large with about

Danielle, Charity and Hope perform Do-Re-Mi. 2013

70 college students attending. I somehow ended up at the end of our tour, and by the time I got inside the classroom, our team member, Daniel, was in the front of the class introducing himself in English. To my surprise my oldest daughter then took the microphone from him and then introduced herself as Danielle. The teacher then invited all of our group members to come up so we each introduced ourselves.

I had the idea of my girls performing a dance for the class. They had learned the song "Do-Re-Mi" from the Sound of Music along with an accompanying dance. After a bit of hesitation, they agreed and went up front together. It was amazing to watch my girls singing and dancing in front of 70 North Korean college students, sharing their talents and culture. The class gave them a resounding applause and my girls returned it with smiles and a bow.

Charity's birthday happened to fall on one of our days in Pyongyang. Our guides suggested we eat dinner at the Turtle Ship Restaurant on the Daedong River. Since we knew it would be difficult to find a cake, my wife had brought Korean Choco Pies, which are snacks similar to Ding Dongs. We headed to the restaurant where our guides sat at a separate table for the meal.

When we got to the gift opening time, the guides presented Charity with a present and we then had Choco Pie cake. There were extras so Charity went around sharing them with the locals and staff who usually don't have the opportunity to have this kind of snack. This seemed to really break the ice, as there had been an unseen barrier between us as foreigners and the locals. Before I knew it, the girls were again performing their Do-Re-Mi act and the ice was broken. Our waitress fired up the karaoke machine and sang their version of "Happy Birthday" to Charity. We then took over the restaurant singing Karaoke and dancing. It turned out to be a really fun party and one of those moments that

Daniel and So-Young dancing at Charity's birthday party. 2013

you think can't happen in North Korea. When all the walls fell down, we were all just people enjoying each other's company and celebrating Charity's birthday together.

The Arirang Mass Games were running that year and we were able to attend. If you have not seen this event, it's quite a spectacle. In addition to tens of thousands of dancers and gymnasts, there is a 20 thousand person human pixel board.

While watching the show, I happened to run into Mr. Park, our first local "surfer" whom I'd met the previous year. I asked if the people holding the pixels ever made a mistake and he said, "No, never!" He was excited to see me though and I asked if he'd ever tried to surf since the last time I'd seen him. He said he was waiting for someone to come and help him learn how and asked if I'd come back to teach him. This question was the first seed being planted for the surf camp idea I'd have later in the trip.

Visit to Wonsan University of Agriculture

Our next destination was the east coast of North Korea, and on the way we stopped at the Wonsan University of Agriculture. Our local tour guide greeted us at our bus in the parking area. At first, her demeanor was businesslike. Her job was to tell us about the university. At one point, our group was standing in front of the main school buildings. There was a special tree in front of the building that had been commented on by all three of the country's leaders, Kim Il Sung, Kim Jong Il and the current young leader Kim Jong Un, during visits to the school.

As our guide was explaining what the leaders had said about the tree, she was staring directly at Hope. The more she stared, the less she seemed to be able to concentrate on what she was supposed to say. Basically this little seven-year-old, bi-racial Korean-American girl looking up and listening to the story about the tree, had totally distracted her. She recovered and was able to finish her talk well. Hope then gave her a big smile and complimented her.

As we continued to walk through the grounds, the guide became more and more friendly and her demeanor softened. At the end of the University tour, she introduced us to her own daughter and we took pictures. It's amazing what a smile can do.

Don't Go Surfing

Later while driving along the coastline, I again saw waves. Nothing really big but it was totally rideable. Yet again I didn't have any gear. On the way to Mount Geumgang, which is near the border with the South, we stopped at Sijung beach for a bathroom break where there were some small waves.

There was a man in the water who was trying to catch a little shorebreak with a blow-up beach ball. If he only knew how much more fun it would be with a boogieboard. While pondering the situation, the idea struck me that instead of traveling to the country with the intention of trying to catch waves, it might be better to introduce surfing to the country. The best way seemed to be to put a surf camp together where locals could be taught how to surf. I thought if we could do it correctly, we might even be able to leave equipment behind in order for the locals to continue on with the sport after our foreign surfers left.

I pitched the idea to our tour guides and asked them to run it by their director whom I'd met the previous year. They did and he accepted the proposal. The problem was I had no idea how to pull it off. I was committed though and would just need to figure out how to make it happen.

The following day, we were again driving along the coast. We were at the exact spot where the previous year we'd seen waves but couldn't stop because the beach was controlled by the military. At that moment I happen to remember an organization I'd met about 10 years earlier in Hawaii called Surfing the Nations (STN).

When I met them, STN was still fairly small but they had big plans to use surfing as a method for creating peaceful relationships between the western world and countries that are often hostile to western culture. They happen to be very successful in Bangladesh where they introduced surfing, helped create a surf club and also run annual surf contests. The possibility of helping me run a surf camp in North Korea seemed to be right up their alley so I planned on contacting them after the trip.

A Day at the Beach

Our group stopped at Wonsan Bay for an afternoon at the beach. As I've seen at many other beaches during the holiday summer season, there were many people out from the city enjoying the beach and seaside. Our guides rented an umbrella from the beach shack and we sat down to enjoy ourselves.

The only problem was that a soccer game between local men was taking place all around us. The action would come right up to where we were camped out, with the locals passionately playing in their skin tight purple beach shorts. The ball would often fly through the middle of our group, stopping only when it hit someone in the head. It was a really interesting and fun experience to watch these men play with such enthusiasm that not even a group of tourists could stifle.

My girls wanted to go down to the shore to build sand castles. When they got to the water, they met several local children and they all played together. It just shows that kids are kids no matter where they come from and given a chance can have a great time together, despite backgrounds and cultural barriers. Later the girls commented that there was no difference between playing with the local North Korean kids as kids from the South. Maybe there is something we as adults might learn from the children.

Hope's popularity apparently extended to the beach as well. The girls wanted to go swimming to cool

Local men play beach soccer in Wonsan. 2013

off so I took them into the water. Hope was still not a strong enough swimmer to go into the water alone so I was holding her and as we were wading out. Then, a local man approached us and said, "Hi, Hopey!" in Korean, which is her Korean nickname. I'd never seen the man in my life but he already knew my daughter because they had met earlier.

Korean culture is distinct from western culture when it comes to children. Koreans are generally more affectionate towards other people's children, albeit in

I find an Angry Birds towel in Wonsan. 2013

an innocent way. They will want to hold, and even kiss kids on the cheek, even when they've only just met. I do my best to understand the culture and my wife and I have done our best to educate our kids. Although they look a lot different than full blooded Koreans, they speak the language and try to honor Korean cultural norms.

So the man held out his hands for Hope to come to him. Not wanting to be rude, since apparently she'd already met him, I let her go. The only problem was he continued wading further out into the water. She was looking at me and began to cry, at which point he turned around and brought her back. It was an odd moment that I never thought would be possible, a North Korean man, a total stranger, was carrying my child out into the sea? Once Hope was back in my arms, everything was okay and we continued to chat with the man. I spoke in simple Korean and Hope did some really basic translation.

Our beach time was drawing to an end so we began to get ready to leave. Someone handed me a large beach towel to dry off, and I was surprised to see it had an "Angry Birds" design. At the time, apparently the game was very popular on the locally built tablet computer. It was another moment showing just how much the doors of North Korea have been opened to the outside world.

Swapping Watches

Although the roads in North Korea are often bumpy, the bus drivers do their best to make visitors feel comfortable. My kids loved the bus rides because there were no seatbelt restrictions. Back home of course, seatbelts are mandatory. Hope and Charity would go to the back of the bus and pretend it was a big trampoline. As we hit bumps, they'd hold onto the two seats furthest to the rear of the bus and get flung into the air. This is likely sounding a lot more dangerous than it was in reality. Of course if it had been, I'd have made them stop. The girls were having a great time and the bus driver allowed them to do it.

A member of our group named Daniel had been adopted from Korea when he was a baby and he grew up in Switzerland. He was in Korea to look into his ethnic heritage. He also was able to connect with our driver and develop a friendship.

Our schedule was to fly back to China the following morning. On the way back to Pyongyang, we were at a rest stop about halfway back to the city. The rest stop is a beautiful scene on a lake. Daniel was sitting with the bus driver on the curb. As they were hanging out, the driver was admiring Daniel's Swiss watch. Daniel noticed the bus driver's watch was probably made in China so he offered to trade. The driver accepted, and with a huge smile on his face, they made the swap. Daniel knew that he wasn't really getting the better end of the trade but really wanted to bless the driver. Of course, it's not often one gets a North Korean bus driver's watch as a souvenir so maybe Daniel got the better deal after all.

The bus driver also seemed happy with the trade. This encounter was another cool point of engagement where people connect person to person. That particular trip was full of those kinds of moments. I've received criticism for taking my family to North Korea, however,

Daniel and the bus driver just before swapping watches. 2013

it was a trip I in no way regret. What an experience my family had together! Not only did we get to see and experience the country, but we had many opportunities to engage with the people of North Korea.

This was the case for everyone in the group. We all enjoyed our time and relationships, especially with our tour guides. Although they are trained to deal with foreigners, tour guides in North Korea are just people like you and me. They genuinely care about their country and wish the best for visitors. Both of our guides cried genuine tears when we left. In truth, we cried too, not only because we were saying goodbye but also for the brokenness of Korea. How long will Korea remain divided? When will we be able to freely see our friends in the North without all of the politics in the way? I don't pretend to think our little group made a dent in the political issues surrounding Korea, however, we did make friends and that's where change really begins, person to person.

Surfing Diplomacy

The Story of Surfing Continues

After I returned home from that trip, I looked up Surfing the Nations online and spoke to their co-founder Cindy. I explained who I was, that we'd met about 10 years earlier and how I hoped they might help me introduce surfing to North Korea. She said they'd been thinking about Korea but figured only the South was open to surfing. Cindy shared the idea with the leaders of STN and we moved forward with planning.

It was hard work to get organized, including my having to travel to Hawaii to meet and talk about details. After a year of planning, on August 1, 2015, actually one year to the day of when I thought of calling them, we were on Sijung beach in North Korea running the first ever surf camp.

The week prior to that first camp in North Korea, I traveled to the northeastern corner for five days with a small group of tourists. This time I took my bodyboard along hoping to finally score some waves. Of course it was totally flat.

We were scheduled to go to a local beach I'd never visited before called ChoJin Bay, a beautiful beach about 15 minutes north of Rajin city. As we bumped along the coast, all I could see were what in surf lingo we call "ankle slappers." It was totally unrideable, even if I'd had a longboard. Surfers say, "Pray for surf" and because it was so flat, that's exactly what I did.

When we got to ChoJin, I was surprised to see that the surf was about one meter, with great conditions. Nothing to get worked up about, but at least it was

My first ever wave in North Korea. 2014

something to ride and a whole lot better than anywhere else I'd seen that day. I had a bodyboard, was in North Korea, and there was small but rideable surf. I'd waited years for this kind of chance so there was nothing stopping me. It was small and mushy, barely enough energy to get going but I did catch my first waves in North Korea that day. Finally! When we got out of the water, I asked our guide to inquire with the local beach shack worker if he had ever seen anybody catch waves there. He responded that he'd never seen anything of the sort. This confirmed that likely, at least for this particular beach, no one had ever surfed there before.

Surfing Is Officially Introduced to the Last Country to Receive It

My trip to the northeastern portion of North Korea came to an end and I returned to China before traveling on to Beijing to meet the team from Surfing the Nations. The group arrived in Beijing and we then flew to Pyongyang on Air Koryo, North Korea's official airline. It's often called the "world's worst airline," but I think that's a bit unfair. I've traveled with many airlines and they are far from the worst.

North Korea traditionally invites all visitors to Pyongyang on a city tour. One of the stops is the war museum. For most people, a museum focused entirely on war might be kind of a downer, because who wants to think about that? It's not necessarily the most fun place to go, but it's a place where I think we have an interesting opportunity for a unique type of impact.

This was illustrated by one of our group members named Stevie. At the museum, North Koreans present their side of history. There are videos, historical photos and exhibits that all serve to illustrate their side of the Korean War.

The video portion is particularly interesting as the history is almost the exact opposite of what Americans learn about the War and national division. Immediately after the video, due to its nature, everyone was a bit tense. In order to break the tension, we had a break at a coffee bar near the video room. While we were enjoying coffee, Stevie approached the local War Museum guide with a few questions. He asked if she had given tours to many Americans and if anybody had ever expressed any apology for the ravages of war. In all the tours she had given, no one had ever expressed any remorse. Stevie went on to tell her that his grandfather had been involved in World War II and that his father had fought in Vietnam. Even though he had not been directly involved in any wars, Stevie said he was sorry for the pain that war had caused her people. She didn't really know how to respond because for her the war was technically still going on and her job deals with it every day.

Even though the guide didn't respond as well as we would have hoped, it was still an engaging moment. Stevie was able to reach across a cultural barrier. He was not required to say what he said. The war happened long before he was born and he was in no way responsible, yet he took the opportunity to try and touch a heart with words of reconciliation.

The First Surf Camp

After our time in the capital, we moved to the coast by bus and arrived at Shijung Beach on July 30 of 2014. The following day, July 31 would mark the first day of the first ever surf camp in North Korea, officially introducing the sport to the last country in the world to receive it. Our camp participants consisted of 12 English-speaking tour guides from the Korea International Travel Company (KITC), which is the largest state-run travel company in the country. One of the KITC directors and the person whom I'd traveled with in 2012, thought it might be best for his guides to experience surfing first so they might be better equipped to guide other surfers into the country in the future. In the process, if they got into surfing then all the better.

This was the first surf camp ever done in the country so the director wanted to be there to make sure everything went well. He's the person who helped our sports cultural exchanges happen. The word "stoked" is typically used by surfers to refer to our excitement about waves. The KITC director also ended up being just about as stoked on surfing as his employees.

The KITC director knew the surfer term "pray for surf" so he asked if I was going to do so. I said of course I'd be praying for surf and he then asked how big the waves needed to be. I said I'd prefer it be flat for the first couple of days so his people could get used to being on the boards. Then it would be good if the waves came up

Surf camp participants installing surfboard fins. 2014

a bit to maybe half a meter so they could get a feeling of the power of the waves. But the fourth day I told him I was praying for big waves so we could demonstrate the full possibilities of surfing.

Our group had brought 10 soft-top surfboards[24] and we had a good time installing the fins and leashes with the participants. It was the first time we were together as a group with the future surfers from North Korea. The great thing about the sport of surfing is how it can bring people together. Before long, we were all pretty excited to be sharing this unique experience.

When we arrived at the beach it was totally flat, like a lake flat. It was fine with us as it presented the opportunity for our participants to get used to the idea of standing up on surfboards in a safe environment. After some basic group instruction by Julie, who was our main instructor, we had our two main guides go out to try standing up. In that precise moment, Mr. Park and Mrs. Kang walked out into the water and into history.

This was the same Mr. Park who had been paddling in 2012, and who I'd run into in Pyongyang the previous year. Since he'd been waiting for someone to come and show him how to surf, and since he was already the first unofficial surfer, I'd specifically requested he be one of the participants. Ryley, our other surf instructor, pushed him towards shore. There were no real waves to speak of, however, Mr. Park stood up and officially became North Korea's first surfer! Mrs. Kang was then pushed by Julie and became the first woman surfer in North Korea. A bit later, Ryley and I were standing on the beach watching our group push the locals on boards and I recall looking at him saying, "The world just changed!" Surfing had come to the last place on earth to receive it.[25]

We woke up on our second day of the camp to find the waves totally flat again. My group of surfers were understandably disappointed, but there being no waves

Mr. Park becomes the first North Korean surfer. 2014

was exactly as I'd hoped. We spent time with the locals refining paddling and pop-up skills, as well as having a relay paddle race. Using surfboards, two teams would race out about 30 yards around Ryley and back to shore where they would hand off the board to another person. Both teams were mixed between the North Korean camp participants and foreigners. It was utter chaos and pandemonium but amazing to witness as it was the first time ever for North Koreans and foreigners to be doing such a thing. I was sitting in the shade near the shore with the KITC director watching this relay race, where everyone is having a great time. There were probably several hundred local people on the beach watching this unfold as well.

As I was sitting there, I heard the KITC director chuckling because the whole scene was totally ridiculous and out of control, not something you'd ever imagine happening in North Korea. I also began to laugh, turned and asked him, "Could you have ever imagined this kind of thing happening in your country?" He replied that he couldn't have and it was great to see.

Fortunately, on our third day the surf began to pick up a bit. We moved up the coast to a beach near Hamhung City called Majon and checked into the Majon Tourist Hotel Villas. This was the same place I'd stayed in 2012 with the people from Waves for Water, and where Mr. Park first paddled a surfboard.

Waves in the Sky

On the morning of the third day, there were little waves about .5 meters high, and by the afternoon we were seeing waves at about a meter. This was exactly as I had hoped. It was really good for our participants as they began to get a feel for actually moving with the waves instead of only being pushed. We ended up calling the spot "Pioneers" or "Gaechokja" in Korean. The spot was named by Mr. Park, which was appropriate because he was the country's first official surfer.

Surf camp participants riding a wave in Majon. 2014

It was exciting to see the locals on real waves, but I was still looking for something else for the final day. For the last day of the camp, I wanted to see a significant swell so we could we fully demonstrate the possibilities of riding waves. At dinner on the third night before last full day of the camp, the KITC director informed us of a typhoon that had crossed over the peninsula. From what was described to us (we didn't have any access to the internet or any weather broadcasts) it sounded very similar to the typhoon that had come through in 2011 where I'd seen amazing waves. I had an idea of what would happen and went out on a limb predicting we'd begin hearing surf start to pound in the middle of the night and by morning there would be a significant swell.

My prediction proved to be spot on and in the morning we arose about 6 a.m. to 2 to 3 meter waves. Again, this was exactly as I'd hoped. All of the surfers jumped out into the surf as quickly as possible. I was the only one up with a camera and had to stay on the beach for the first session to document the scene. Interestingly enough, the first guy to surf a legitimate wave on the trip was a Swede named Stefan Eriksson. Later when our photographer came down to the beach I grabbed my bodyboard and jumped out. By that time, it was about 8 a.m. and there were probably several hundred local people watching us, which was really cool because my desire was to see as many local people as possible exposed to the possibilities of surfing.

A little later in the morning, an interesting thing happened in the clouds called "Kelvin Helmholtz Instability"[26] where the tops of clouds get sheared off by wind, which creates a pattern of waves. This phenomenon is fairly rare in the Northern Hemisphere and nobody in our group had ever seen it. As we were surfing, and all the locals were on the beach watching, this phenomenon occurred with a pattern of about 15

Me on a decent size wavein Majon. 2014

wave-shaped clouds in the sky right in front of where we were surfing.

When one of the locals saw the waves in the ocean and in the sky, he mentioned to one of the STN members, "The man upstairs must be listening to your prayers." I don't know if he really believed this but the very fact that he said it was interesting to hear. It was a really amazing moment.

The waves were biggest in the morning and by the afternoon were in the 1 to 2 meter range. Although it

Waves in the sky. 2014

still had a bit of size and power, the drop in size allowed our local participants to get in the water and really get a feel for the power of the ocean. Some did better than others with at least one guy making it out to the surf line-up. He was really excited to have made it. It was actually comical because it took him 45 minutes to get out but just after he did, a set wave came and he was gone, pushed into shore. He did try to make it out again but ended up surfing the white-water inside, which was probably a good call.

Stevie catches a wave on a blow-up trutle. 2014

There were a couple of other memorable moments from the afternoon. One would be when out of the corner of my eye I spotted a local man running down the beach to join us with a raft and swim fins. I guess he'd borrowed them from the hotel and wanted to try catching waves. Unfortunately, the hotel had cordoned off a space for us to surf and the staff told him to move down the beach a ways. We watched to see how he would do, and he ended up using the raft as a boogie board. Not realizing the raft wasn't the best tool for

Chris shares a surfboard with a local boy. 2014

the job, he did try to stand up a couple of times but of course he didn't have much luck. I remember thinking that wave riding in North Korea had officially just become a "local" thing.

Another memorable moment occurred when Stevie asked some locals (in broken Korean) to borrow a turtle raft from them. He had previously seen it in a hotel beach shop and had wanted to catch a wave on it. The locals reluctantly handed it over and Stevie then proceeded to catch a wave. It was pretty surreal watching this American surfing a turtle raft inside North Korea.

On our last day of camp, we had another amazing moment where just after we took a group photo, the STN leader rallied everyone together into a big circle suggesting we all put our hands together as a sign of unity and peace. As we did, he led us in a shout as together, Europeans, Americans and North Koreans shouted "For peace!" It was such a memorable moment that I had to question whether it was actually happening. Those kinds of moments aren't "supposed" to happen in North Korea. In fact, it did happen and that's exactly what we had gone there to do, to try our best to bring peace to the Korean Peninsula, even if only in a small way. Based on these experiences, we believe surfing is a great tool to bring people together.

Surfing Brought Peace to My Country

The experience didn't only have a deep impact on our group but also on the local surfers. One of our first surfing participants was a KITC guide I'll call Lee. Most of the time Lee was a fairly serious guy. Throughout the surf camp we called him "Mr. Juche" named after the word that describes their official ideology of self-reliance. You might say Lee was an evangelist. Two of our foreign surfers spent the entire camp with him, and he continually preached that they should believe in the Juche idea. My guys were really nice about it but would share that they had a different ideology than he did. They understood he had his ideas and respected them but didn't share his beliefs.

On the last night of the surf camp, we had a beach barbecue with all of our participants. All of our foreign surfers brought the people they had shared surfing with all week to the front and encouraged them. They'd share all the good things they'd seen in them over the week. I think it's fair to say North Koreans don't likely experience this kind of thing often, especially with foreigners.

As Lee got up, my two guys encouraged him by telling him how they appreciated his passion for his country. Lee then said he wanted to say something. Again, normally a serious guy, he smiled and shared how all week while surfing he'd felt so peaceful. He never thought he'd see the day that foreigners would bring a sport like surfing to his country. He concluded by saying, "Surfing brought peace to my country." Personally, I was really shocked that this serious guy experienced peace through surfing. It was pretty amazing.

There was a blog online not too long ago posted by a guy who'd traveled to North Korea with KITC, the same tour company. In the post, the author showed a photo

Mr. Lee with Stevie and Graham after sharing his heart. 2014

of himself with Lee looking very serious. In fact, he looked so different I was wondering if he was the same guy from the surf camp. So I pulled out some photos to compare and it was definitely him, but he certainly didn't look like the guy who had such a peaceful week surfing with us.

I happened to run into Lee at the Pyongyang airport on a later trip. As I was walking in the door, he was right in front of me and looked serious as usual. I greeted him and reminded him of how we'd gone surfing together 2014. When I mentioned surfing, his face totally changed and he smiled widely, recalling how much fun he'd had. I told him I was planning on coming back the following summer and I hoped he could join us for surfing again. He replied that he'd love to.

We said goodbye and about 10 minutes later I saw him with his group by the check-in counter and his serious look had returned. I was keeping tabs on my group, making sure they were all getting checked in and walked by him again. I said "Lee, I really hope we can go surfing again together." His smile returned and he said he also hoped it would happen. Surfing really can be a useful tool for touching hearts and lives.

Surfing Diplomacy

On the way back to the capital after the camp, the KITC director and I were on the bus talking about how things had gone. He'd learned to surf along with his employees and had a great time. He'd also heard what Lee had said about surfing bringing peace to his country and observed how the foreigners had interacted with his people. We were discussing the possibility of continuing to do more camps in the future and I asked him if he remembered back in the seventies when the United States and China used "ping-pong diplomacy" as a tool to normalize their relations. He did recall the term so I mentioned we should do "surfing diplomacy"

First surf camp crew on the beach in Majon. 2014

between his country and mine to bring peace. Without pausing, he looked at me and agreed we must do it.

True engagement takes place when we can agree to disagree and yet maintain a friendly relationship. Unfortunately, people often confuse and conflate this kind of "engagement" with "appeasement." In a political context, appeasement is the making of concessions in order to avoid conflict. The word engagement is used here in a diplomatic sense similar to that of "ping-pong diplomacy" used in the 1970s

to improve relations between China and the United States.[27] Although both countries considered the other as its enemy, sports engagement was used as a tool to change each side's views of each other.

If we only see North Koreans as enemies, we can never see the situation change. This is not to say the current atmosphere on the Korean Peninsula is one of peace and friendship, but rather that the atmosphere can definitely be improved, if we begin to look at each other differently. This can happen through using

Making friends with a local teenager in Majon. 2014

methods of engaging North Korea in order to improve the relationship. Methods for engagement such as humanitarian aid, business and sports are equally as valid in North Korea today as they were back in the 1970s. Yong Kwan Kim and John L. Crompton best sum this up:

> A key to the changed political relationship between China and the United States was the opening of the former to tourists in 1978 and the encouragement of cultural and scientific exchange groups, conferences, and sport groups. While it may be overly-optimistic to expect that the World Tourism Organization's motto, "Tourism: Passport to Peace: will be shared by everyone in the two Koreas, it would be a step in the right direction.[28]

Abraham Lincoln was famously quoted when asked by a critic why he advocated treating Southern rebels with respect. The critic pointed out that since they were the enemy, they should be destroyed, to which Lincoln replied, "I destroy my enemies when I make them my friends."[29]

We need to engage in order to see improvement. Pressure from the outside to change seldom works. The future of the international community's relationship with North Korea will ultimately depend on how well we know them. If they are open for us to come into their country, then of course we should go. At the same time, we need to accept that we go into North Korea on their terms. When we do, while also building relationships, we'll see the terms begin to change.

When I visit North Korea, I like to teach them the urban language term "frenemy," which is a combination of the words "friend" and "enemy." My message to them is that if we all put in the effort needed, we can turn the situation from being "enemies" to "frenemies" and then finally to being friends.

The international community does itself a huge disservice by not taking advantages of current opportunities for engagement. To quote Felix Abt, who is a business affairs specialist on North Korea:

> If you have no presence in the country you cannot influence anything for the better. I have seen that you can talk with people and influence them and help change minds. What's the alternative to engagement? You want to nuke them, you want to isolate them so people starve to death? The best thing in my view is to support market forces to invest and engage. Market forces are the strongest agent of change. We should work with everybody. We should work with ordinary people and with the government.[30]

Sanctions and other outside pressure will not accomplish all the changes needed to see improvement of the situation between North Korea and the rest of the world. Instead this will only happen if all sides persevere with a desire to improve the relationship.[31] This is already taking place, largely from foreigners visiting the country, maybe not in huge ways but at least in small incremental ones. At the core of all the issues surrounding North Korea and the Korean Peninsula, is relationship. It's the key to improving the situation. As it was with ping-pong diplomacy, engagement with North Korea today remains the best way in which we can see peace on the Korean Peninsula.

Since the first surf camp, we have been able to do a lot of things inside North Korea because the manager from KITC believed in what we were doing. It's amazing what we can actually do in North Korea today, and I really appreciate how hard he worked to make it happen from his side. Although we haven't yet seen "surfing diplomacy" used as a tool on government levels, we've continued to use surfing as a way to promote sharing culture and creating peace since that very first surf camp. In my humble opinion, it would be amazing to see surfing diplomacy or any other kind of sports diplomacy used as a tool to exchange culture and bring peace between nations.

Sharing Our Culture

Surfing in the Pyongyang Water Park

Surfing is not only limited to the ocean. When I heard they opened up a water park in Pyongyang, I wanted to see if they had a wave pool where we could surf. Before leaving the capital for the first camp, one of our guides showed us a short video clip on his phone from which we saw it had a small one .5 meter wave and might be surfable on a soft-top surfboard. Unfortunately, we ran out of time on our schedule and we had to move on to the coast so we could not see it in person.

I was disappointed but figured we'd try again the next year. For the following surf camp in 2015, we set up a surfing demonstration at the water park. My plan was to travel to North Korea again with my family. Because we had just been in South Korea while they had been experiencing a Middle East Respiratory Syndrome or M.E.R.S. outbreak, we couldn't go into North Korea unless we stayed in a non M.E.R.S. country for two weeks. This was in order to make sure we were clear of the virus. We got the notification we were unable to go to North Korea about 12 days before we were scheduled to fly out. We already had tickets to China though and had blocked off the time. Instead of canceling the tour completely, we met the Surfing the Nations group in Beijing where I conducted the briefing before we sent them off to North Korea.

Even though I could not be there, all the planning I'd done worked out. They were able to go to the

Sharing surfboards with locals in the wave pool. 2015

Pyongyang Water Park and do the first ever surfing demonstration in the wave pool. The electricity was out and the wave pool was not working when they got there, so they were unable to immediately do any surfing. At the very least, they were able to get local people on surfboards, and then when the electricity came back on, they were able to do a short demonstration.

The pool was very crowded, but the locals made space so our surf team could catch waves. Each time a team member had a good ride, the crowd erupted into

Ryley demonstrates surfing in the wave pool. 2015

cheers. The tour guides even got into it and were able to catch some waves. They told me that although it was a short excursion and somewhat chaotic, still they were able to do the demonstration and show several locals how to surf.

I intentionally set this up because the Pyongyang Water Park might possibly be the best spot to expose surfing to the nation, as many of the elite families are able to go. There certainly were no big waves but it was definitely an epic moment in surf history. The goal was

Wes demonstrates skateboarding in Pyongyang. 2015

to continue with the idea of "surfing diplomacy" and show what might be accomplished when surfing brings people together.

The group had a skate demo set up for the next day at the Pyongyang Inland Skate Park. Our skaters were able to demonstrate skateboarding skills and then offered some gear and instruction to the local kids. Unfortunately, all the gear had to be given back in order to be donated to the inline skate club. Even though both our group members and the local kids were a bit

Kaylen shares skateboarding with a local girl. 2015

disappointed, they understood the gear could be shared by others as well.

After their time in the capital, the group moved on to Majon beach on the east coast, the site of the second surf camp. Unlike in 2014, this time the group was able to actively recruit people off the beach. Along with the initial camp participants who came from Pyongyang, two local teenage girls joined and learned how to surf. One of the great things about the camp was one of the guides not only became friends with these two girls but ended up acting as their surf teacher. As part of the camp, our group also introduced skimboarding[32] (skimming on a board on wet sand) as a new beach sport and were able share it with the locals. Unfortunately, the waves were uncooperative for much of the week with several flat days.

Others Catch the Wave Too

The third surf camp in North Korea was also run in August, 2015, but by a completely different group. The camp location was at the Majon Hotel located on the bay just south of the Majon Villas near the city of Hamhung. The team leader was Nik Zanella, a coach for the Chinese National Surf Team in Sanya City, Hainan Island in China. He reported they got surf in the 1 meter range one day, and overall the camp was a success. According to a recent article, on the website

The Inertia,[33] Nik was planning to run a surf school at the Majon Hotel. There weren't many details provided, however, the tour company he was working with planned on offering surf tours to North Korea from 2016 and beyond.

Sharing Boogie Boarding With a Local Boy

I'd spent my two weeks in China to make sure I had no M.E.R.S. symptoms. Unfortunately I'd missed the second surf camp, but was able to visit Rajin in the extreme northeastern corner of North Korea. The main purpose of this trip was for well drilling not surfing. During my visit, the company we worked with had a beach party for all the employees and I was able to go to a beach I'd never been to.

I had brought a small boogie board to give to my co-workers and when we got to the beach, I noticed one of the company employee's son was a natural in the water. His dad said whenever they went to the beach, the boy was "like a fish" and never wanted to get out of the water. One of my fellow-foreigner co-workers had taken the boogie board out and was trying to jump into tiny waves. The boy was watching intently and absolutely curious about this idea of riding the board. I saw an opportunity and asked if he wanted to try. He accepted my invitation without hesitation and I began pushing him into waves.

It's been said that one of the most exciting things a surfer can experience is not the actual act of riding waves but seeing the excitement on the face of a kid when he catches his first one. I don't know if this is true for every surfer but it was definitely true for me. Seeing the smile on this boy's face, even on those tiny waves, made every trip I've made to North Korea worthwhile.

The boy's dad had been watching from the beach. He seemed excited about what his son was doing. I later asked him if he'd like to try wave riding while standing

I share boogie-boarding with a local boy near Rajin. 2015

up. He replied he didn't know anything about how to do it but if he had the chance he'd give it a try. I'd love to one day see surf gear in the hands of locals like this dad and his son.

The Fourth Skate/Surf Camp in 2016

My dream the previous year for surfing in the water park had come true, but I was really disappointed to have missed it. Because the water park is in the capital I felt like it was an important place to do surfing as it's where you would imagine the influencers hanging out. If we could show them surfing, it would be a unique way to impact people with a new sport. It would be something new and cool for their country. So I asked whether we could do it again, but have some time blocked off in the wave pool to really do a proper demonstration. Happily, the water park management said yes.

Our surf group returned to Pyongyang in August of 2016 for our third full-fledged trip running a surf camp into the country. We had our surfers and four solid skaters who did their best to get whoever they could on skateboards. We also brought a b-boy who wanted to introduce b-boying, more popularly known as breakdancing to North Korea.

Straight off the bus in Pyongyang, the skaters had a bellman from the Yanggakdo Hotel on a skateboard. It was hilarious to see this guy trying to skate in his bellman uniform. He tried it though and seemed to have a blast. Our skaters would continue to do this kind of thing for the entire trip.

I didn't think we could top the previous year of having done the first ever surfing at the Pyongyang water park, but somehow we did. We pulled up at the water park and got all the boards ready. The management then asked all the local people to exit the pool and gave us time to do a proper surfing demonstration. After that, we were able to invite locals to try surfing.

A local stands up on his first try in the wave pool. 2016

Our guys had the pool to themselves for about 20 minutes, where they traded off catching the small waves. We had a group of about 50 locals watching and they seemed fascinated. My best guess is none of them had ever seen surfing before or had any idea it was even possible.

As the demo was winding down, Stevie pulled a local guy out of the crowd, gave him literally 30 seconds of instruction, pushed him into a wave and he stood upon his first try. Excited, he immediately got a couple

Ryley gives surfing instructions. 2016

more waves. This inspired a few other locals to try it and we were off and running, sharing surfing in a wave pool in Pyongyang, North Korea.

In the beginning, only a few local men were willing to give it a shot. That is until one brave middle-aged woman decided it was her turn. She didn't actually stand up but instead rode on her belly to shore. After she got her ride, it seemed everyone else thought, well if she could do it then so can I. We got literally mobbed and it just turned into this totally chaotic

Pushing locals into waves in the wave pool. 2016

time of boards flying everywhere and people's bodies flying everywhere, it was pretty insane. Finally, our surf instructor, Ryley, called a time out and asked our tour guides for the pool to be cleared so he could give the crowd some basic instruction and establish a bit of order.

After getting the crowd out of the pool, Ryley spent about 10 minutes doing basic surf instruction on the pool deck, with one of our guides translating. Afterwards we went back into the pool and formed a line with the locals being pushed into waves one by one. As one of the only people in our group who spoke any of the Korean language, I ended up being the one pushing people into waves. In my limited Korean, I'd tell them after I pushed them, they should count to two and stand up. We set up a rotation with a line of people and boards. This system seemed to work really well and in total our group had upwards of 50 locals on surfboards.

Eight nations were represented in the wave pool that day including, Finland, Switzerland, Sweden, United Kingdom, Canada, The United States, Russia, and of course North Korea. The KITC director was again with us and when he realized there were so many people from different countries in the wave pool we heard him say, "Wow, surfing really makes peace!" After maybe 30 minutes of pushing people into waves, the wave park manager wanted to open up the pool to the rest of the park patrons so we shut down the surfing. We ended the time with a splash battle with the locals. The whole experience made up for my missing the previous year.

It was awesome to see that we can be from different places in the world, from different backgrounds, and with different ideologies, but we can come together and use surfing as a tool to promote peace. With the exception of my group and a Russian diplomat's daughter, I really had no idea who the rest of the local

Sharing the surf culture. 2016

people were. I don't know if there were any top level people from the country, but if they were there, then I think they got exposed to something that can indeed make peace. If we could have eight different nations surfing in the Pyongyang wave pool, then isn't anything possible? If ping-pong diplomacy worked between China and the United States in the 1970s, then why not surfing diplomacy with North Korea today?

Surfing Continues to Grow

Since our time in the wave pool was so successful and the locals were so stoked, the park manager asked KITC if they could leave a surfboard behind. Their intention was to experiment and do some research as to whether they might bring more boards to the park. KITC agreed and clearly we were happy to see it happen. I don't know for sure, but I can just see the pool workers taking the board out after hours to catch a few waves of their own.

After our time in Pyongyang, the team traveled again to the east coast of North Korea, to Majon beach near the city of Hamhung. We had eight local North Koreans, five women and four men join us as the main participants. The KITC director again asked if I was going to "Pray for Surf." Of course, I agreed and explained that I basically wanted to see the same thing happen as had happened in 2014. I got my wish and the first two days were totally flat, so we did a lot of pushing and practicing pop-ups.

Since our group was having such a good time surfing, it's natural that locals began to show interest. We were again given permission to pull people off the beach to surf. Whenever this happened, our local North Korean participants became the teachers, inviting people to come over, showing them how to pop-up and then pushing them into small waves. It was amazing to see how the passion for surfing can be so easily shared.

Our third and fourth days on the coast took us to another beach hotel where we saw a bump in the waves. On the third day, it was still pretty small with only .5 meter surf, but it gave our gang a feeling of actually catching waves with a bit of power. You could see the excitement on their faces as they were able to feel the surge of the ocean under their feet.

This particular beach had seen surfing already as Nik Zanella had run a camp there the year before. Nik left a few longboards and a stand up paddle board or SUPs behind and one of the local lifeguards had continued to surf. I started calling him "The Captain" because he looked so official in his beach outfit. We were able to give him a cool surfing trophy, which made his day, or maybe even his year.

Our fourth and final day on the coast dawned with beautiful conditions and a waist to shoulder high waves. We had planned on getting up at dawn to be able to surf early because the temperature was going to be in the high 90s Fahrenheit by mid-day and our "surfer chicks" as we had begun calling them, refused to go outside in that kind of heat. We had an amazing morning, as we watched our North Korean friends begin to really get the hang of wave riding. Up to this point, we'd been pushing them into every wave, but several of the women as well as the men were starting to catch waves on their own.

"The Capitan" receives a surf trophy. 2016

One of our North Korean surfers had been feeling sick and missed out on some of the surfing. As she started feeling better, even though it was 98 degrees, she asked Ryley to take her surfing. I took a photo from the hotel room just after Ryley pushed her into what was essentially the first real wave she'd ever caught. I was really impressed with her for going for it even when she wasn't feeling well.

Late afternoon saw a slight decrease in the size of the waves, but the good conditions held up and a ton

Local surf camp participant catches her first wave. 2016

of people were both on the beach and in the water. One local teenage boy was swimming, and he asked some of our guys in Korean to let him try to catch a wave. They got the idea and gave him instruction in English while he was on the board. They pushed him into a wave and watched as he promptly popped up and rode it to shore. We were lucky enough to get it on video. On his second wave, Ryley was surfing next to him and gave him a high five midway to shore. One thing I know for sure is this local teenager will not easily forget that day when a group of foreigners shared surfing with him.

We didn't know this but the hotel restaurant chef had been on the beach watching us the day before. The next day, I was pushing our participants into waves and happened to look over only to see the chef catching a wave. He'd seen everyone having such a good time the day before, so on his break decided he wanted in on some of the action. Seeing him out there really blew me away. In only three years, surfing in North Korea was now a reality.

During the planning for that trip, I was contacted by a Brit named Louis Cole who was interested in joining the group with his friend Lane. I'd never heard of him but found out he was well known on YouTube as a travel vlogger.[34] North Korea had been on his bucket list so he was excited to come with the hope of documenting the trip for his YouTube channel. I was a bit hesitant as it constituted a risk on my part if he were to come and do some sort of "hit-job" video. My requirements were that he not focus on any negative aspects of the country but instead focus on how we are able to engage local people. He agreed and along with Lane, joined the group.

Once the trip was over and we were back in China, Louis then began uploading his daily vlogs to YouTube. On around the third or fourth day of his uploads, the media began to take notice and Louis was accused of being paid by Pyongyang to make propaganda videos.[35] Let me be very clear, Louis was not paid to make videos. I was not and am not being paid by the North Korean government either. Louis did not travel with the intention of creating propaganda for their government. Instead, we traveled with the intention of running a third annual Surfing the Nations surf camp, as well as sharing our culture. Louis happens to be an amazingly talented vlogger and videographer and joined to document his adventure. In fact, it was so unplanned our guides didn't know what to make of this tall dude with dreadlocks pointing his camera at himself all the time.

Other than KITC, who facilitated our tour and surf camp, nothing was "staged" by the North Korean government for Louis to make videos. Of course, we did travel the tourist route, especially in Pyongyang, which many others have been on, and adhered to the preset itinerary.

Certainly I've experienced times in North Korea when things seemed to be staged. One time while visiting a local kindergarten, there were several little girls wearing traditional dresses, all made up for our visit. I never got the feeling that they were trying to deceive us in any way, they just wanted to show us their girls were cute and could dance. Unless you are visiting a show, such as the children's palace where it's obviously well-rehearsed (it's a show), at least for my groups, things tend to be very organic. Whether in the capital, the countryside or the beach, the people you see in Louis' videos are real local North Korean people living their normal lives.

It was difficult for Lane and Louis to give skateboards away. Although they tried, our guides told them it wouldn't work. As we'd learned the year before, gifts need to be given in a group context. Louis ended up giving skateboards to the tour company for distribution to a local school. A couple of the guides got into skateboarding so he asked them to keep a few for themselves too, which was really cool.

One other really interesting aspect to this story is Louis and Lane were able to make a music video, something that was totally unplanned. Lane had sampled a beat from a Korean traditional gayageum stringed instrument at a local restaurant in Pyongyang. From there he wrote a song titled "Surfing in the DPRK" and asked one of our guides, Ms. Lee, to write a chorus in Korean. He also convinced her to record the chorus as well as to appear in the video. Every aspect of this process was organic and unplanned, yet they were able to make a music video inside North Korea.

Some in the media still suggested Louis' vlogs were North Korea propaganda, I think this is vastly missing the point. The very fact Louis could even make the videos at all with no pre-approval, interference or screening by the North Korean government is

Ms. Lee catching a wave. 2016

what's most telling. Others, such as VICE[36] may have had different experiences and I cannot comment on their challenges and obstacles. What I can say Louis' experience was about as organic as it gets, which is truly amazing.

Lasting Impact

The Magic of Bubbles

In 2017, just prior to the travel ban that prevents Americans from entering North Korea, we ran our fourth consecutive surf camp. Like all the rest, this most recent camp was full of engagement with local people through a third surf demonstration at the water park and even greater numbers of locals surfing at the beach.

Before heading to the coast, we were having lunch in one of the restaurants in Pyongyang when we got the opportunity to go to one of the capital´s smaller skateparks. The skaters took their boards to the skatepark while a few others from our group who didn't skate walked to a grassy area. One of the girls named Josefine had some bubbles in her purse that she'd brought from back home in Sweden. She had hoped to use them earlier in the day when we'd visited a school, but we never really got a chance to play with the kids.

At first, they didn't see any kids playing in the park, even though it was more of a playground than a skate park, but as they got to the grass they saw two kids playing. When Josefine approached and saw a brother and younger sister, she remembered the bubbles in her purse and started to blow some towards the two kids. Her goal was to catch their attention and not scare them away from a group of foreigners. It worked, and after a few minutes of the kids popping bubbles, the little girl was blowing bubbles so that her brother could catch

Josefine sharing bubbles. 2016

them. Joy radiated from their faces, as Josefine and the kids played and shared a special moment together. Those two kids have forever earned a place in Josefine's heart.

Where Are You From?

On the third day of our 2017 surf camp, we were at the Majon Tourist Hotel Villas. As we were surfing some small waves with our camp participants, we saw couple of local young men rowing towards us in an inflatable raft. They were curious as to what we were doing and watched for several minutes before our team member, Anthony, convinced one of them to abandon the raft for a chance to try surfing.

After a couple minutes of instruction through broken Korean and hand signals, Anthony got the young local on the surfboard ready to be pushed into his very first wave. A small set of waves was on the horizon so Anthony let him know that he'd soon be pushing him into the wave and to be ready to stand up. With a little push, he caught the wave and stood up. He was super excited and regardless of the obvious language barrier, the smile on his face told Anthony all he needed to know.

The young man caught three or four more waves before finally asking, in what little English he knew, where Anthony was from. Anthony said he was from

America and was a friend. When he said that, it was like a switch flipped and the young man's entire demeanor changed. His face became blank with what looked like disgust and confusion.

In North Korea, from a very young age, kids are educated that Americans hate them and want to see them dead. They really do not know anything else since this is the only message they get. So, here was this American man who was sharing surfing and calling him a friend. I was watching this take place and could see the guy was confused, yet he kept on surfing. Anthony continued to encourage him after every wave and kept calling the guy his friend.

Eventually, as though to make sure he heard right the first time, the guy again asked Anthony where he was from. Anthony repeated that he was from America then asked me the Korean word for friend. I told Antony the word in Korean was "chingu," and so Anthony said, "I'm American. *Chingu!*" Again as if a switch flipped, the man's face changed and he looked disgusted.

The young man approached Anthony two more times with the same question and two more times Anthony said, "I'm from America, I'm your friend." Every time his answer was met with the same confused and disgusted look, and yet we continued to cheer him on as he caught waves.

AND OTHER STORIES FROM INSIDE

We got up the next morning for breakfast and I ran into Mr. Jay in the restaurant. He looked really unhappy. A bit later in the hotel lobby, he told me the tour company had replaced him and that he could not go to the coast with us, but that we would have another guide for the remainder of the trip. Immediately I thought about what had happened the day before and went and told him I was sorry if my group had caused him any trouble, and that I would look forward to seeing him again the following year. I then gave him a big hug.

Mr. Jay at the skate park. 2016

215

Everyone else in the group took turns giving him hugs, as well and telling him how much they had enjoyed the short time we'd been together. He was crying by the end and I know he really felt we truly loved him. We said goodbye and his replacement introduced himself.

I'll call the replacement guide Mr. Chung. He was a serious guy, not really laid back at all, and basically the exact opposite of Mr. Jay. I hoped if he spent enough time with us, maybe he'd loosen up a bit.

It took a while but by about the third day of our surf camp, he paddled into a wave on his own, stood up and rode it to shore. When he stepped off the board, he had a look of triumph on his face. He did a fist pump and after that moment was a lot less serious. Catching that wave really changed his view of our group and he seemed to understand why we were there. It wasn't about anything other than sharing life and the amazing sport of surfing.

On our last night, Mr. Chung gave a speech on the bus about how even though our governments have differences, when we come together and connect as people to people, there is great power in it. He'd seen through our group just how that was possible.

I never forgot about Mr. Jay though. All through the next year, I was hoping and praying we would have him again as our guide for the next surf camp. When I took a group for skiing and snowboarding in February of 2017, I asked about him and was told he was still with KITC. With the summer and our fourth surf camp approaching, I continued to hope and pray we would be able to see him again.

We landed in Pyongyang on August 1, 2017. We were passing through customs when one of my group members, Stevie, looked over and said, "We got Mr. Jay." As I heard this, I was really overcome with happiness that we'd get another chance to share surfing with this guy. After clearing customs, I was finally able to say hello and tell him how happy I was to see him again.

Later that day, we stopped at a local souvenir shop and I asked Mr. Jay how he happened to be with our group again. He said he didn't understand it, that he thought he'd never get to be with our group after what had happened the previous year. He explained that he'd just finished with another group a couple days before we arrived and was supposed to have had three days off. Then after only half a day off, he was called into the office and told he'd be with our group the following day. He said he was really shocked but so glad for the opportunity to see us again. Those of us who had been there the previous year told him how happy we were he was with us.

We continued on with the trip and Mr. Jay was able to have the chance to learn how to surf and finish what he'd not been able to finish the previous year. When we were saying goodbye at the airport, I told him that due to an upcoming travel ban by my government, I did not know how long it would be before I could come back. I said I hoped it would be sooner rather than later. I also took the opportunity to look into his eyes and said, "I love you brother" and gave him a big hug. I didn't expect this at all, but he replied, "I love you too." Even though we are separated by culture, politics and now a travel ban, I believe what he said. In the end, what my dad modeled for me has proven to be true, even in

Mr. Jay catches a wave. 2017

North Korea. We are all brothers and sisters and need to fight against the things that separate us and for the things which bring us together.

Culture as a Tool for Engagement

During our trips, we've seen many opportunities for engagement and sharing life and culture with local North Korean people. Over the past several years, we've seen literally hundreds of local people on surfboards, skateboards and skimboards. From the capital to the countryside, my teams have been able to interact with many local North Korean people. The greatest part of all this was seeing these locals share what they were experiencing with others. What tremendous opportunities we have had to exchange our culture, as well as to love and care for every-day North Korean people!

On one trip, one of our women team members was hanging out on the beach with our local surfer girls and they were chatting about how our group was different from others who had visited their country. All of the girls participating in the surf camp were tour guides and have extensive experience hosting visitors to their country. They told our team member there was a difference between our group and other visitors. They further explained the reason, "It's that you care about us." While other groups usually only travel to North

Korea to see the country and check off a mark on their bucket list, we had come to share our lives with them.

In the brief time, since we have been able to introduce surfing to the people of North Korea, the sport seems to have been well accepted. Although it is still in its infancy, surfing is now officially part of their tourism industry. A few of the KITC guides who participated in our camps have continued to surf whenever possible.

We ran into one of the participants from the first camp and asked him if he was surfing regularly. He said there had been some times when he had been asked to guide other surfers and was even able to take his son surfing. He said, "After I go surfing, I lay awake in bed thinking about catching the next wave."

Even though we still cannot freely explore the coastline as we'd like, and the surf spot options are limited, we look forward to the day when peace finally arrives on the Korean Peninsula and the entire coast opens up. For now, even though things are moving slowly towards more access, the fact remains that the doors for surfing in North Korea are open. It even appears that this "sport of kings" will remain part of their beach culture. I feel blessed to have been a part of seeing surfing introduced to the last place on earth to receive it and am looking forward to seeing how it evolves. Who knows what's possible? If we could introduce surfing to North Korea, then isn't anything possible?

Peace First Policy

Whether sharing surfing, drilling wells, distributing rice, coal or lanterns, all the work I've done in North Korea has been for one real purpose, which is to work towards peace and eventually the unification of the two Koreas. When thinking about the idea of national unification, we have to first ask the question: How do we get to a place of peace on the Korean Peninsula? There are what we can call small scale problems, which given enough time, might be solved between the two Koreas prior to a peace treaty. However, there are three main issues which are a hindrance to ever getting a full-scale peace accord. These three issues prohibit peace from ever becoming a possibility and all serve to keep the Peninsula in a perpetual state of war.

The first issue is the most politicized: North Korea's nuclear program. The reality is sanctions that have been implemented have not prevented North Korea from obtaining nuclear capability. If sanctions were designed to prevent this capability, we can say they have been a colossal failure. As much as the international community might wish otherwise, this is the reality we face. The international community has to deal with the situation as it is.

At present, both the current U.S. and South Korean administrations are able to say they have been handed the issue, but they also must deal with it as it is. How do we get to peace? A "Peace First" policy would be the best way forward. With this policy, North Korean, U.S. and South Korean administrations would make peace a priority, and then solve the major issues from a position of peaceful relations instead of a position of war.

In dealing with the nuclear issue, both the U.S. and South Korean administrations would put peace

Ryley trades hats with a local man. 2016

first and then work with the North to solve the issue of denuclearization of the Korean Peninsula. With a peace accord in place, the North wouldn't need to argue for nuclear weapons as a defense.

The second biggest obstacle to peace in Korea is the issue of U.S. and U.N. armed forces on the Korean Peninsula. Annual joint military exercises between the U.S. and South Korea are an ongoing source of tensions, and the North sees them as a prelude for invasion. Thus, the traditional position held by the North is all foreign armed forces must vacate prior to a peace accord being put into place. The only way for this issue to be resolved is for the North Korean administration to put peace first and then work with the U.S. and South Korea to solve the issue of foreign armed forces on the Peninsula.

The third major hindrance to peace in Korea is the issue of National Unification of the two Koreas. Each side has traditionally held to their differing view of unification as a prerequisite to a peace accord. The result being the Peninsula in a perpetual, official state of war, with both sides facing each other across the DMZ, 24 hours a day, seven days a week, 365 days a year, for decades.

So what is the solution? Again the solution is to put peace first. Put a peace accord in place between both Koreas, and then solve the issue of national unification with both sides working together towards a model upon which all Koreans might agree. This may take 10 years or more to solve. It would not be too big a stretch to say most people in Korea would prefer 10 years or more of peaceful relations, with the possibility of unifying, to another decade of both Koreas being officially at war.

Solving these issues will require compromise on all sides. The U.S. and South Korea would need to compromise and prioritize peace in order to solve the nuclear issue. The North would need to compromise and say peace first in order to solve the U.S. and U.N. armed forces issue. Both Koreas would need to compromise and commit to peace first, and then work together towards national unification.

In the words of Kim, Yong Kwan Kim and John Crompton, "For reunification of Korea to occur, both sides need to confront at the official level their mutual fears and jointly look for ways of redefining areas of conflict so that they become amenable to solution. To this point, this has not occurred."[37]

Putting peace first may sound simple but history has clearly shown it's not all that easy. All sides will need to recognize that "simple" and "easy" are two different things, but nothing worth doing is ever easy. It's going to take hard work and compromise on all sides. If a peace accord could be put into place and these three major issues could be solved, it would be amazingly worth the hard work. If all sides could make the necessary policy shifts towards a peace first policy and decide to do whatever it takes, peace is absolutely within reach on the Korean Peninsula.

Our experience introducing surfing is only one example of what is possible when we put peace first. The political world might do very well by looking at what NGOs and humanitarian organizations have already been able to accomplish inside North Korea as a model.

A New Narrative is Needed

Until recent years, North Korea has been a very isolated country. Although they welcome visitors, the country still faces many challenges. Life for many in the countryside or provincial cities is difficult. Travel in the country is controlled and local people need permission to move outside of their designated living and work areas. Traveling outside of the country is typically reserved for the wealthy or well-connected, though I have been very surprised at the number of people I've met who have legally visited China.

Although we have seen greater and greater access, North Korea is also not yet open to the point where foreigners can visit on their own terms. Today you are not going to be able to land in Pyongyang, rent a car and drive around at your leisure. Tourism takes place under controlled circumstances, hence groups have official guides, are not allowed to wander off the beaten path, and have to strictly adhere to a preset itinerary. The good news is that tourists are given more and more latitude every year. This can only be seen as a good thing.

I've been focusing on the positive changes going on in North Korea. Of course the country still experiences difficulties, examples of which the reader can find in other works. While we should not ignore the challenges every day North Koreans face, we need to be aware of the fact that the country is in a process of slowly opening its doors. Although it is shocking to me how fast North Korea is opening, it's not opening as fast as the international community would like-a fact commonly reflected in the current international media narrative. As North Korea is slowly opening, many good things are happening in the country, leaving the international media narrative largely outdated.

Mass starvation is not happening as in the 1990s and early 2000s. A market economy has been emerging for years and has really accelerated its growth in the past five.[38] Agricultural and manufacturing reforms have been enacted by the North Korean government, giving both farmers as well as factory managers greater incentives.[39] Long-term impact of these reforms remains to be seen, however, they are a step in the right direction. The number of prisons, as well as the number of prisoners, has been reduced in recent years.[40] With all we still do not know about the true goings on in the country, we should still be cautiously optimistic. None of this is to say we should ignore other important issues, however, we should be willing to give credit where credit is due. At the very least, current reforms could be a starting point for dialogue.

A major problem lies in the fact that the international media narrative surrounding North Korea is centered on conflict. If you watch the news, or what might be more aptly described as "entertainment news," this is generally the case, but especially so regarding news about North Korea. Anything reported on North Korea is reported in an "us" vs. "them" manner. These attitudes on the part of the news media cause many positive developments inside North Korea today to go under reported, or more often than not, completely ignored.

In addition, works being done in North Korea by NGOs, business people, and even tourism, which do not match the "us" vs. "them" narrative, are labeled as crazy. The media will either cast you as being pro-North Korea or Anti-North Korea with no middle ground ever recognized. As a result, people working in North Korea tend to fly under the media radar simply to avoid being labeled as nut-jobs.

Yet, in spite of the negative narrative, good things are happening inside North Korea. This should be good news and the international media would do all parties a great service by taking a more balanced approach. A more realistic and current narrative needs to be adopted, which would be conducive to bringing about peace in Korea. Unfortunately, this is a tall order for a news media addicted to conflict. It's my hope that the experiences shared in this book might help to update that narrative. Until peace is finally and fully realized in Korea, I'll continue to do my best to be a peacemaker in the land.

I'd like to say a special thank you to my lovely wife for pushing me to write this book. Without her encouragement, it would never have happened. Also thanks to Derek Schoenhoff for believing in it, even though North Korea is such a controversial topic. Thanks to Diane Talbot-Schoenhoff for helping with the editing. My big sister Jamie Bauer also deserves thanks for giving me honest and needed feedback and helping iron out the final wrinkles. Last but not least, I want to thank the many people I have worked with, both in and out of North Korea, without whom none of the stories shared in this book would have been possible.

Endnotes

1. *Note:* The majority of readers may not be familiar with the formal name "Democratic People's Republic of Korea" ("D.P.R.K."), but instead might be better familiar with the informal name "North Korea." For the most part, I will be using North Korea for the remainder of the book.

2. "Donald Trump: N Korea's Kim Jong-un a 'smart cookie'," April 30, 2017, video, 1:27, from an interview televised by CBS on *Face the Nation.* Accessed June 19, 2018. http://www.bbc.com/news/world-asia-39764834

3. Jethro Mullen. 2017. "How North Korea makes its money," *CNN Money*, April 5, 2017. Accessed June 19, 2018. http://money.cnn.com/2017/04/05/news/economy/north-korea-economy-china-trump-xi/. *See also* Evelyn Cheng, "Five ways North Korea gets money to build nuclear weapons," CNBC, April 18, 2017. Accessed June 19, 2018. http://www.cnbc.com/2017/04/18/how-does-north-korea-get-money-to-build-nuclear-weapons.html.

4. Joseph Margulies. 2016. "This Is the Real Reason Private Prisons Should Be Outlawed," *Time Magazine*, August 24, 2016. Accessed June 19, 2018. http://time.com/4461791/private-prisons-department-of-justice.

5. "Part1: Point-in-Time Estimates of Homelessness," *The 2016 Annual Homeless Assessment Report (AHAR) to Congress,* U.S. Department of Housing and Urban Development, November 2016:8. Accessed June 19, 2018. https://www.hudexchange.info/resources/documents/2016-AHAR-Part-1.pdf.

6. Le Miere, Jason. 2017. "North Korea War Would Be 'Catastrophic,' and 'Worst in Most People's Lifetimes,' U.S. Defense Secretary Mattis Warns" *Newsweek*, May, 28 2017. http://www.newsweek.com/north-korea-war-us-mattis-616943.

7. Alton, David and Rob Chidley. 2013. *Building Bridges: Is There Hope for North Korea* (Lion Books, 2013) 10.

8. Kim, Yong Kwan and John Crompton. 1990. "Role of Tourism in Unifying the Two Koreas," *Annals of Tourism Research* 17:365. http://agrilife.org/cromptonrpts/files/2011/06/Full-Text61.pdf.

9. Flake, Gordon and Scott Snyder. 2003. *Paved With Good Intentions: The NGO Experience in North Korea* (Praeger Publishers 2003) 94.

10. Jasper, Daniel. 2017. "Engaging North Korea Vol. II: Recommendations from 65 years of humanitarian engagement" *American Friends Service Committee* June 2017. Accessed June 19, 2018 https://www.afsc.org/engagingNK_vol_ii.

11. "Useful Idiots" Urban Dictionary, May 23, 2017. Accessed June 19, 2018. http://www.urbandictionary.com/define. php?term=Useful%20idiot.

12. As of August, 2017, American Passport holders are banned from traveling to North Korea unless they obtain special permission from the United States State Department. "United States Passports Invalid for Travel to, in, or Through the Democratic People's Republic of Korea" Wednesday, August 2, 2017 *Federal Register* 82:147:36067.

13. *See* www.krahun.com.

14. Flake and Snyder, *Good Intentions* 72.

15. Wilson, Brian and Mike Love. 1963. "Catch A Wave" *Surfer Girl* The Beach Boys (Capitol Records 1963).

16. Weiland, Ben. 2012. "Surf Guide to North Korea: Images Captured By Satellites From OuterSpace Pt. 2," Arctic Surf, July 9, 2012. Accessed June 20, 2018. http://www.arcticsurfblog. com/2012/07/surf-guide-to-north-korea , 2012

17. Blakemore, Erin. 2017. "North Korea's Devastating Famine," history.com 2017. Accessed June 19, 2018. https://www.history. com/news/north-koreas-devastating-famine.

18. Flake and Snyder, *Good Intentions*, 31.

19. Ibid., 33.

20 Ibid., 39.

21. Ibid., 64.

22. "W4W North Korea," November 2012, video, 3:10, Posted by "Waves for Water." https://vimeo.com/59748313.

23. "Barbie and Ryan tour to the DPRK," October 24, 2013 video, 2:11, Posted by "abarbieplace." https://www.youtube.com/watch?v=gjosLHJZMpA.

24. US sanctions against North Korea currently prohibit Americans from donating sporting equipment as they are considered luxury items. The European contingent of our group had brought the surfboards, which they intended to leave behind as it was not in violation of their respective country's laws to do so. It now seems likely that US sanctions will in the future be relieved, which would make it much easier to conduct these kinds of sports culture exchanges.

25. "First Ever Surf Camp in North Korea," August 21, 2014, video, 5:42. Posted by "LNKM." https://vimeo.com/103995428.

26. Paperin, Michael. 2006. "'Kelvin Helmholtz Instability' Cloud Structure," April 2006, Brockman Consult. Accessed June 19, 2018. http://www.brockmann-consult.de/CloudStructures/kelvin-helmholtz-instability-description.htm.

27. Colley, Rupert. 2011. "China, America and the Soviet Union: 'Ping-pong diplomacy,'" *The Cold War: History In an Hour* (WilliamCollins 2011).

28. Kim and Crompton, *Tourism,* 361.

29. Fisher, Dennis. 2012. "Changing Enemies Into Friends," *Our Daily Bread*, July 2012. Accessed June 19, 2018. https://odb.org/2012/07/26/changing-enemies-into-friends.

30. Evans, Stephen. 2015. "A Quiet Revolution In North Korea," *BBC News*, January 14, 2015. Accessed June 19, 2018. http://www.bbc.com/news/business-30812237.

31. Alton and Chidley, *Bridges*, 131.

32. Skim Editor. 2017. "The First Skimboarder in North Korea," September 7, 2015, skim.co. Accessed June 19, 2018. http://skim.co/new/the-first-skimboarder-in-north-korea.

33. Hernandez, Juan. 2015. "North Korea is Open for Surf Tourism." The Inertia. Last modified Tuesday July 28, 2015. Accessed June 19, 2018. https://www.theinertia.com/surf/north-korea-is-now-open-for-surf-tourism.

34. Cole, Louis (FunForLouis). 2016. "I'M ACTUALLY VLOGGING THIS! - North Korea Day 1," August 10, 2016, video, 12:48. Accessed June 19, 2018. https://www.youtube.com/watch?v=VmCpTzA6SKc&list=PLecf3E7ybgfEeea9rGUAfsHrSimUL1woG.

35. Lawson, Richard. 2016. "YouTube Stars Are Now Being Used for North Korean Propaganda" Vanity Fair, August 16, 2016.

Accessed June 19, 2018. http://www.vanityfair.com/culture/2016/08/louis-cole-vlogger-north-korea.; Douglas Ernst, "British YouTube star posts videos from North Korea: 'Bro, we're here!'" The Washington Times, August 16, 2016. Accessed June 19, 2018. http://www.washingtontimes.com/news/2016/aug/16/north-korea-enlists-british-youtube-star-louis-col.; *See also* Shelby Carpenter, "Meet The YouTube Star Who Loves North Korea, Human Rights Violations Be Damned" Forbes, August 16, 2016. Accessed June 19, 2018. https://www.forbes.com/sites/shelbycarpenter/2016/08/16/meet-the-youtube-star-who-loves-north-korea-human-rights-violations-be-damned/#759d2ea8d735.

36. Smith, Shane. 2011. "Inside North Korea," The Vice Guide to Travel, video, 20:35, December 19, 2011. Accessed June 19, 2018. https://video.vice.com/en_us/video/vice-guide-to-north-korea/56815b6132382b833c2230ad.

37. Kim and Crompton, *Tourism* 358.

38. Lankov, Andrei. 2017. "What's on Kim Jung Un's Mind?," Aljazeera, March 9, 2017. Accessed June 19, 2018. http://www.aljazeera.com/indepth/opinion/2017/03/kim-jong-mind-170308124321267.html. *See also* Eric Talmadge, "North Korea's Creeping Economic Reforms Show Signs of Paying Off," *The Guardian*, March 5, 2015. Accessed June 19, 2018. https://www.theguardian.com/world/2015/mar/05/north-korea-economic-reforms-show-signs-paying-off.

39. Lankov, Andrei. 2014. "Reforming North Korea," Aljazeera, November 30, 2014. Accessed June 19, 2018. http://www.aljazeera.com/indepth/opinion/2014/11/reforming-north-korea-20141117121917871925.html.

40. Kwang Jin Kim. 2012. "Camp 22 Disbanded on Defection Fear," Daily NK, September 28, 2012. Accessed June 19, 2018. http://www.dailynk.com/english/read.php?catald=nk01500&num=9865. *See also* Lankov, Andrei, "The Surprising News From North Koreas Prisons," Bloomberg, October 13, 2014. Accessed June 19, 2018. https://www.bloomberg.com/view/articles/2014-10-13/life-beyond-north-korea-s-gulag. *Also* "Democratic People's Republic of (North) Korea," World Prison Brief, May 30, 2017. Accessed June 19, 2018. http://www.prisonstudies.org/country/democratic-peoples-republic-north-korea.